GREAT FOOD FOR KIDS

Jenny Chandler

weldon**owen**

CONTENTS

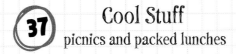

The Kids' Intro

Cooking is one of the most useful, rewarding, and fun things that you'll ever learn to do. Whether you hope to become a rocket scientist, play football, teach music, or win an Olympic gold medal, one thing's for sure, you'll always have to eat. When you can make your own food, the whole business of eating becomes much more exciting and enjoyable.

Food is so important; it's not just about grabbing a snack every time you feel bored or even feeling full at the end of a meal, it's about fueling your body with the right food so that it runs like a well-oiled engine. When you're young, the body has so much to do; you're constantly learning, growing, and running circles around all the adults in your life. You've probably heard people say "you are what you eat," and it's pretty true. If you eat lots of junk food and sugar, you won't have as much strength and drive to do all the challenging things in life. Don't worry, this certainly isn't a diet book: it's not full of strict rules to follow, but there will be plenty of healthy food facts along the way.

Being adventurous in the kitchen gets you trying lots of different ingredients, and the more variety we have in our diets the better. Every fruit, vegetable, fish, or whatever else you choose to put on your plate has a different mix of the vital calories and nutrients that we all need. So, get out there tasting and discovering new foods and eat to thrive, not just to survive.

The great thing about cooking is that once you've mastered a technique you can create all sorts of variations. Start with a simple key recipe, then move on to the other suggestions in this book and finally, once you're really confident, add your own touches too. A meatball could be Italian-style with spaghetti, Moroccan-style with couscous, or Vietnamese-style with a spicy dipping sauce. It's up to you to decide. There are plenty of options and ideas for many of the recipes in the book; that's because we don't all like the same things and so you can tailor-make a dish to suit you, your family or friends.

As well as enjoying yourself, when you prepare a meal you'll earn lots of brownie points around the house too. Grown-ups love to have a day off, or in some cases they might not be well enough or have the time to cook, so this is your moment to step in and shine. Imagine inviting your friends over for a meal you've cooked: with a bit of practice you'll be able to. Just remember to let an adult know when you plan to cook and don't leave the kitchen looking like it's a disaster zone or you might not get invited back!

You may start out needing quite a bit of adult help with some of the recipes, but you'll soon be cooking up a storm. Be sure to read the safety pages: cooking can be dangerous if you're not on the ball.

This book is filled with real dishes, not children's food: stuff that you'll still love making when you're a teenager, a student, and for many years to come. So what are you waiting for?

Let's get going with some REAL COOKING.

And a Few Words for the Adults

Great Food for Kids aims to inspire and teach children around the seven-to-thirteen age group, although there's nothing to stop you from making the recipes with younger siblings or even using the book for some inspiration yourself.

Learning to cook at a young age has so many benefits: it instills a love of real food that can last a lifetime and provides the building blocks of a vital skill that many adults sadly still seem to lack. Understanding where food comes from, and the difference between processed junk and home-cooked meals, helps create healthy eating habits. It's also fun, and a perfect time to engage and share a common interest with a child.

Children are often hesitant to try unfamiliar ingredients, which is not surprising; we are hardwired to be suspicious of new foods. Our hunter-gatherer ancestors didn't want their kids tasting every berry they came across; it was a matter of survival. Thankfully, as we grow up our inquisitive nature, along with peer pressure and a more relaxed attitude towards eating, usually takes over. It's in our interest to eat a really varied diet. Time and time again I see kids overcoming their fears and hang-ups about a certain food when they prepare it themselves. Including a new ingredient in a familiar mix is an excellent way to start; such as zucchini in a stir-fry, or beets in an ever-popular chocolate muffin.

Most recipes in this book have a simple basic version allowing kids to learn a technique. Once they are familiar with the technique, then it's great to move on to a variation. This builds confidence and independence as they begin to go it alone. Once a child can make "The Cake" they can transform the result with some minor tweaks: they've mastered the recipe; have the right cake pan; they know it will work.

The emphasis of this book is on tasty dishes that children and their families will enjoy eating together rather than elaborate party food. There are some treats, because children love to bake sweet things; but there are many more healthy dishes too: it's about building a balance without creating any sense of deprivation.

Children will require different levels of help and supervision depending on their age, their familiarity with the kitchen environment (I've met nine-year-olds whose kitchen skills would put many an adult to shame), and the particular dish they're cooking. For this reason I've not graded the recipes by difficulty; only you can gauge how much assistance your young cook might need. You may begin by cooking the recipes with your child but try to give them some ownership of the dish, allowing them to choose variations and encouraging them to taste and season the food.

When we invite children to help with shopping, to enjoy cooking, and to take pride in their results, they'll not only become more adventurous with their choices, they will relish their food too.

BE SAFE

Read through the recipe with the cook and work out where they may require assistance. Knives, heat, and electricity all pose real dangers but by familiarizing yourself and your child with the blue "Getting Started" pages you can create a safe environment. Always be on hand when kids are cooking; you never know when they will need you.

GETTING STARTED: SAFETY FIRST

There seem to be lots of rules, but once you're
in the habit of working safely in the kitchen
you won't need to read them every time.

ALWAYS LET AN ADULT KNOW WHEN
YOU'RE PLANNING TO COOK.

Cooking can be great fun, but there are plenty of
potential hazards. Have a good look at the recipe
before you start. Together you can work out,
depending on your age and experience, how much
help or supervision you will need when using
sharp, hot, or electrical equipment.

When you see this symbol in a recipe:

!!!!!!

it means beware – time to call an adult to help.

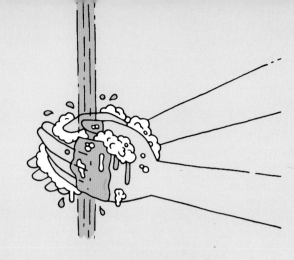

KEEP CLEAN AND TIDY

○ Always WASH YOUR HANDS before you begin. Germs can contaminate your food and make people ill.

○ TIE BACK LONG HAIR; it can get in the way or, worse still, end up in the food.

○ WEAR AN APRON when stirring and frying. It will keep your clothes clean, as well as protect you from hot splashes.

○ CLEAR THE WORK SURFACE so that you can be really focused.

○ GET EVERYTHING YOU NEED READY for the recipe: that's all the equipment and every ingredient. There's nothing worse than finding that you're missing a vital piece of the puzzle once you are halfway through.

○ WASH CHOPPING BOARDS, EQUIPMENT, AND HANDS BETWEEN JOBS and wash especially well after preparing raw meat and fish.

○ KEEP A BOWL NEXT TO YOU AS YOU WORK for all your scraps and trash. You'll feel organized and calm. Empty the bowl into the trash can when you've finished.

○ WIPE UP ANY SPILLS OFF THE FLOOR, or your kitchen can become like an ice rink.

○ Don't forget to CLEAR AND CLEAN UP PROPERLY.

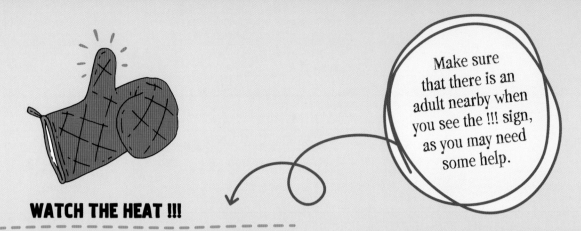

Make sure that there is an adult nearby when you see the !!! sign, as you may need some help.

WATCH THE HEAT !!!

○ ALWAYS USE OVEN MITTS OR POTHOLDERS; towels can get caught in doors or drag in the food. Use oven mitts or sturdy potholders whenever you place something into or take something out of the oven.

○ STEAM CAN BURN, so take great care when opening the oven door or taking the lid off a pan. Always use oven mitts or potholders.

○ HOLD ONTO A PAN HANDLE WHEN STIRRING so that the pan is stable and doesn't tip over.

○ Metal spoons get very hot so ALWAYS USE A WOODEN SPOON FOR STIRRING over the heat.

○ TURN PAN HANDLES AWAY FROM THE EDGE OF THE STOVETOP where you or anyone else might knock into them.

○ CALL FOR HELP WHEN LIFTING HEAVY, HOT PANS AND DISHES.

○ HAVE A SPACE READY FOR HOT DISHES and cake pans when you bring them out of the oven. This needs to be heat resistant so you don't scorch the work surface.

BE SWITCHED ON !!!

○ ASK AN ADULT'S PERMISSION BEFORE USING ANY ELECTRICAL EQUIPMENT; you may need some help.

○ ALWAYS DRY HANDS BEFORE PLUGGING IN OR SWITCHING ON – wet hands could lead to a bad electric shock.

○ NEVER PUT YOUR FINGERS ANYWHERE NEAR THE BLADES OR WHISKS OF ANY ELECTRICAL APPLIANCE.

○ SWITCH OFF AND UNPLUG any electrical equipment before taking it apart to wash.

USING KNIVES !!!

LEARN TO USE A SHARP KNIFE WITH SOME ADULT HELP. IT'S SAFER THAN USING A BLUNT KNIFE WHICH CAN SLIP MORE EASILY.

USE A KNIFE THAT IS NOT TOO LARGE OR HEAVY IN YOUR HAND. A PARING KNIFE (THE BLADE IS ABOUT 4 INCHES LONG) IS A GOOD ONE TO START WITH. YOU CAN USE BIGGER KNIVES AS YOU BECOME MORE CONFIDENT.

FOCUS
No music, no chat, no fooling around; you really do need to concentrate. Your fingers are not on the ingredient list.

HOLD THE KNIFE LIKE THIS

HANGING ON TO YOUR FINGERS

BEFORE YOU GET STARTED

- FIND A SURFACE THE RIGHT HEIGHT – just below waist height is ideal. It might be the kitchen table rather than the work surface.

- DON'T STAND ON A RICKETY STOOL; you could fall with your knife. You will need a solid, wide step if the work surface is too high.

- WEAR SHOES (not sandals or flip-flops) when you are cooking. They will protect your feet if you drop a knife or any hot food.

- Always CHOP ON A FLAT, STEADY CUTTING BOARD. If your board moves around, then put a neatly folded kitchen towel underneath to hold it in place.

- TRY NOT TO CARRY KNIVES AROUND THE KITCHEN; if you need to carry a knife, keep it at your side, pointing down to the floor.

- NEVER PUT A KNIFE, BLENDER, OR FOOD-PROCESSOR BLADE INTO A SINK OF WATER; you might forget it and then cut yourself. Wash the blade and store it safely right away.

THE "BRIDGE" POSITION

The bridge position is used for cutting rounded foods. It's good to cut them in half, giving you a flat surface so that food doesn't wobble around dangerously as you slice.

Put a tomato upside down on its flattest side. Make a bridge with your hand by putting your thumb on one side of the tomato and your fingers on the other. With the blade facing downwards, chop through to the board.

THE "CLAW" POSITION

Use your gripping hand like a claw for slicing and chopping. Fingers and thumb are always curled under, never flat where they could be chopped accidentally.

Try practicing with a green onion – chop off the root, remove the outer skin and then slice the green onion. Slowly move your "claw" back along the onion as you slice. Try keeping the tip of the knife on the board.

Now try practicing with larger vegetables, such as cabbage.

A good time for a vegetable stir-fry?

CHOPPING AN ONION USES BOTH THE "BRIDGE" AND THE "CLAW" POSITIONS

BRIDGE Slice the onion in half and then peel off the skin.

CLAW Now you can SLICE.

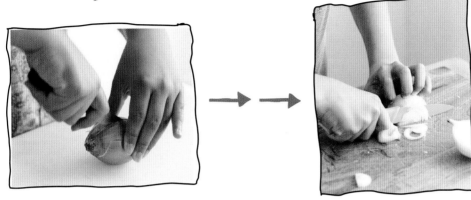

TO DICE:

BRIDGE Make vertical cuts through your onion half down to the board. Don't cut through the root as it holds the onion together.

CLAW Then slice across the onion to make tiny dice.

PEELERS and **GRATERS** are sharp too. Make sure that you have a steady cutting board to work on and watch your fingers and knuckles.

How to Shop

Farmers' markets are ideal places to find really fresh, local food.

Market vendors sometimes have samples for you to nibble — go ahead, it's often a great chance to experience new tastes and flavors.

Fruit and vegetables are at their best when they are grown outside and freshly harvested, so stock up on seasonal treats such as summer berries, autumnal root vegetables, or winter nuts.

If you go on vacation, a visit to the local market is an exciting and colorful way to catch a glimpse of a different culture. How about a "spot the weirdest ingredient" competition? Will you dare to taste it too?

Try the market challenge

See if you can cook a whole meal with ingredients produced or caught within 50 miles of your own home. This could be something as simple as a summer salad with cheese or a complete main course and dessert.

A trip to the supermarket is fun if you get involved. How about making your own shopping list for a recipe from this book?

Look out for simple, natural ingredients. Processed foods have long lists of ingredients, with all sorts of unpronounceable names; they are usually best left on the shelf.

Dairy Food

Dairy foods contain protein (needed for growth and repairs) and calcium (to keep our bones and teeth strong) and plenty of great vitamins and minerals. Some delicious dairy products such as ice cream and cheese are quite fatty. It's really just a question of not eating too much of them, too often.

Any food that's made from a mammal's milk is a dairy product. Most of our dairy foods come from cow's milk but there's goat's and sheep's milk too. Oh, and don't forget buffalo; their milk is made into creamy mozzarella cheese.

THE AVERAGE DAIRY COW PRODUCES OVER 35 PINTS (ABOUT 20 LITERS) OF MILK PER DAY.

Cheese – what exactly is it?

Making cheese was an ancient way of preserving milk. Most cheesemakers purposely add bacteria, among other things, to help curdle the milk (splitting it into curds and whey). They drain off the whey and then the curds usually get chopped up, salted and pressed into a cheese. The bacteria get to work as the cheese ages and mold is encouraged to grow on it too! Sounds weird, but it's oh-so-good to eat!

WEEKS OLD
Very fresh or young cheeses are creamy and lightly flavored like mozzarella.

MONTHS OLD
Older cheeses have more flavor such as Cheddar. Mild cheddars may be three months old, medium about six months old and sharp-tasting mature cheese up to a year old.

YEARS OLD
Intensely tasty. The most famous aged cheese is Parmesan which is often about two years old.

Make your own butter

This is super easy, but you'll need tons of energy and plenty of patience. Half-fill a jam jar with room-temperature heavy cream. Put the lid on tightly. Get your favorite funky music on and dance, and dance, and dance.

shakin' that jar, shakin' that jar

After about 15 minutes you will have a lump of solid, yellow butter floating around in the watery milk. Drain off the "buttermilk" (great for soda bread or pancakes), spread your butter on some toast and RELAX – you'll need to.

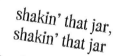

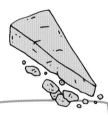

WHAT HAPPENED THERE?
You made the fat globules in the cream stick and clump together until they formed a ball, leaving the watery buttermilk behind.

15

Spice Up Your Life

One small spoonful of spice can work like magic, transforming a simple dish and bringing a whole new world of flavors into your kitchen.

Spices are usually the roots, bark, buds, or seeds of an aromatic plant while herbs are the leaves. Some are used fresh but most are dried.

ginger

cinnamon

cloves

nutmeg

mace

star anise

OUR OBSESSION WITH SPICES SPARKED THE AGE OF DISCOVERY

Over 500 years ago, European countries sent explorers out in search of new routes to the spice-producing countries of Asia, in a desperate attempt to control the trade. Vasco de Gama sailed around the bottom of Africa to reach India while Columbus traveled west and discovered the Americas.

THERE'S NOTHING NEW ABOUT SPICES

Cumin and coriander seeds were used by the ancient Egyptians. Pepper was once so valuable that people used it to pay rent and taxes, as well as using it in their cooking. It still is the most widely traded spice in the world.

They even found some seeds in Pharaoh Tutankhamun's tomb.

A Simple Spice Store

There are dozens of fabulous spices to cook with, but buying lots of jars can be expensive, so a few basics and a couple of good spice mixes are a great place to start.

These are the go-to spices that we use in this book...

SWEET SMOKED PAPRIKA
is made from smoked, dried peppers and tastes of Spain. Be sure to buy the sweet one.

BLACK PEPPER
has fruity flavor and some spicy heat. It's best to grind it rather than buy it as a powder because its flavors disappear quickly.

CUMIN
has a warm, nutty flavor and is especially good in Mediterranean, Mexican, and Indian dishes.

RAS-AL-HANOUT
spice blend will bring wafts of the Moroccan souk into your cooking — it's really good with lamb, chicken, and couscous.

CURRY POWDER
is ideal for Indian dishes. Start out with a mild curry powder (some of them are fiery hot). Most mixes are based upon turmeric, cumin, coriander, ginger, and chile.

GINGER AND CINNAMON
are warm and powerful spices used in both sweet and savory dishes.

CHILE
can be bought as a ground powder, dried flakes, or whole fresh chile. Just remember to GO CAREFULLY.

The hottest part of a chile is the white pith that holds the seeds

The capsaicin in chile actually irritates your mouth or skin (a sensation that feels like burning). It does seem pretty bonkers that we actually enjoy eating it.

There are hundreds of types of chile, some hot, some mild, so always check them out — too much heat can ruin a dish.

Cut off the tip and touch the flesh; now lick your finger. If it is hot and tingly you are dealing with rocket fuel so WATCH OUT, don't use too much.

The world's hottest chile is the Carolina Reaper. It's 500 times hotter than Tabasco sauce (which is already pretty HOT). AAAAAAAAARGH! Where's the yogurt?

Too hot? If you're gasping then take a gulp of milk or a spoonful of yogurt; capsaicin doesn't dissolve in water so no amount of the stuff will wash it away.

Taste and Flavor

So, what makes food taste good?
Your tongue is covered in tiny taste buds which pick up on...

sweet

sour

savory (umami)

bitter

salt

Some say that there should be a sixth point for creamy/fat too.

You don't need to use all the tastes at once to make food exciting. When you season food, you are balancing different points of the star. If there's too much of one element, such as sweet, it can be overpowering, so add a bit of salt or sour and everything works.

Seasoning your food is a balancing act, so always add salt, sugar, lemon juice, etc., a tiny bit at a time and TASTE.

Play with your taste buds

Try little pieces of tomato with one taste at a time.

A tiny bit of...
salt (salty – a little obvious, I know)
olive oil (bitter and creamy/fat)
balsamic vinegar (sweet and sour)
Parmesan (salty and umami)

Now try the tomato with the lot – salt, oil, vinegar, and Parmesan. You've just made a dressing! If that dressing is balanced it will make the tomato's flavor sing.

The more sugar and salt we get used to eating, the less we taste them. Just a small amount of either will work like a highlighter pen making flavors come alive – you don't need too much.

Smells Amazing!

Your tongue is only a tiny part of the picture; the pleasure you get from food actually comes mostly from your sense of smell.

There's the sensation as you sniff the air — those are nasal odors, and then there are the smells you pick up in your mouth called retronasal odors.

Aaah, that soda bread smells good as it's baking.

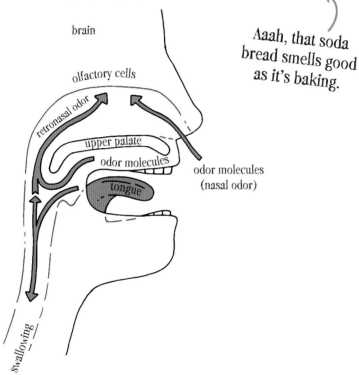

brain

olfactory cells

retronasal odor

upper palate

odor molecules

tongue

odor molecules (nasal odor)

swallowing

We use our other senses too as we're eating

SIGHT

We do "eat with our eyes"; you're more likely to dive in and try something if it looks scrumptious than if it looks like a dog's dinner.

FEEL

You may love or dislike foods because they are slimy, lumpy, creamy, or chewy. A dish is great with a mixture of textures, such as crispy pita chips with creamy guacamole.

SOUND

It sounds crazy but scientists believe that if you play atmospheric music you can appreciate your food more. Playing swishing wave sounds and seagull calls will supposedly make your seafood taste more fresh and fishy.

Cut out the smells and you won't even know what you're eating. Believe me, or better still try out this experiment – it's a very good excuse to eat potato chips!

⭐ Put two different flavors of potato chips in identical bowls, then get someone to move the bowls around.

⭐ Hold your nose, and don't let go until the experiment is finished.

⭐ Taste the chips. What flavor are they?

⭐ Keep holding that nose. Taste again but this time let go of your nose while each chip is in your mouth.

WOW, you'll suddenly be hit by a wall of flavor!

What happened there?

First you could only pick up on the salty or sour TASTES of the chips but then, when you let go of your nose, the air wafted the smell (odor molecules) up the gap at the back of your mouth to the olfactory nerves and BINGO, you got the flavor.

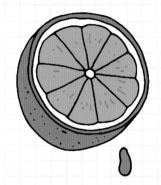

Kick-Start Your Day

tasty breakfasts and brunches

Homemade Granola

MAKES 8 GENEROUS SERVINGS

It's time to make your very own breakfast cereal. You can put your favorite nuts, seeds, and fruit in or change the combination each time to keep things fresh and interesting. It's a great moment to use up leftover fruit and nuts from the kitchen pantry too. Yummy for breakfast with milk or yogurt or just sprinkled over a bowl of fresh fruit.

Adult help for stovetop and oven cooking

4 tbsp coconut oil
  or 3½ tbsp butter

½ cup (150 g) honey, maple
  syrup, or light corn syrup

3½ cups (300 g) rolled oats

1 cup (150 g) nuts
  (raw, not roasted or salted)

1 cup (100 g) pumpkin seeds
  or sunflower seeds

1 cup (150 g) dried fruit,
  diced

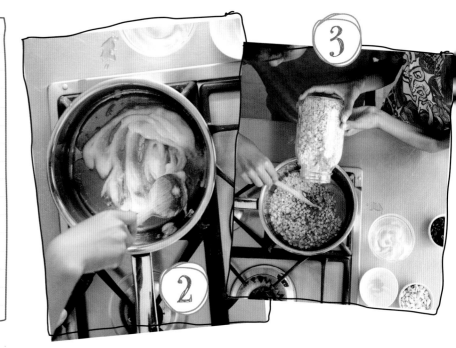

1 Preheat the oven to 300°F (150°C).

2 Put the oil or butter and honey or syrup into a large saucepan.

3 Now heat the pan until the oil or butter has melted and then stir in your oats, nuts, and seeds until everything is well mixed.

4 Line 2 baking sheets with parchment paper and divide the sticky oat mixture between them. Spread the granola out so that it can toast evenly.

5 Bake in the oven for about 30 minutes. Stir every 10 minutes so that the granola gets evenly toasted.

Once golden, remove from the oven and let cool.

6 Stir in the dried fruit and then package into paper bags (for granola to go!) or store in an airtight container for up to 3 months.

Nuts About Nuts

Take your pick from almonds, pistachios, Brazil nuts, hazelnuts, pecans, or macadamias.

If you have a nut allergy, or you're taking the granola to a nut-free zone, just leave the nuts out and add a few extra seeds; the mix will still be great.

Tutti Frutti

How about raisins, dried cranberries, or coarsely chopped dried figs, dried apricots, dates, or dried sour cherries?

A bag of granola is ideal for an instant energy boost on long hikes or bike rides – that's why it's sometimes called "trail mix."

Try

adding 2 teaspoons vanilla or almond extract to the honey and butter mixture at the beginning of the recipe.

Try

stirring a good pinch of ground cinnamon or ginger into the oats for the last 5 minutes of baking.

Try

sprinkling toasted sesame seeds or toasted coconut flakes into the granola once it is ready.

23

Scrambled Eggs

SERVES 2

bad joke

Once you've cracked these eggs everyone will want you to prepare their breakfast — the secret is not to overcook them.

This recipe is so quick to make that it's best to cook just four eggs at a time; it's difficult to cook the eggs evenly if you have too many in the pan.

4 eggs

salt and pepper

1 tbsp butter

toast, to serve

1 Crack the eggs into a bowl or measuring cup and whisk them together with a fork. Sprinkle with a pinch of salt and a grind of black pepper. Make your toast now, if you're having some!

2 Put half of the butter in a small non-stick saucepan or frying pan and place it over low heat. Once the butter is melted and frothy it is time to pour in the eggs.

3 Keep the heat low and stir the eggs slowly with a wooden spoon.

4 When about three-quarters of the egg has thickened and set (this will only take a few minutes), take the pan off the heat. The rest of the custardy-looking egg mix will continue cooking.

5 Stir in the remaining butter. You can add other flavorings at this point (see p. 26).

6 Serve right away on toast or with bagels, blinis, soda bread (see p. 122), or pancakes (see p. 30).

What flavors will you choose?

More ideas for scrambled eggs on next page ➝ ➝

A flat-ended spoon is great for getting into the corners.

Posh Scrambled Eggs

Great for brunch or simple suppers.

1 x Scrambled Eggs recipe (see previous page) + one of these ideas...

Smoked Salmon and Dill

4 slices of smoked salmon

4 sprigs of dill

1   Slice the smoked salmon into thin ribbons and take the feathery fronds of dill off the tough stalks.

2   Stir most of the salmon and dill into the scrambled eggs along with the butter once you remove the pan from the heat.

3   Decorate with the rest of the salmon and dill, and serve.

Ham, Cheese, and Chive

2 slices of ham

1¾ oz (50 g) hard cheese such as Cheddar, Emmental, or Gruyère

2 tbsp chopped chives

1   Slice the ham into strips and grate the cheese.

2   Add the ham, cheese, and most of the chives to the scrambled eggs at the same time as stirring in the remaining butter once you remove the pan from the heat.

3   Sprinkle with the rest of the chives and serve.

Spinach and Parmesan

a large handful of spinach leaves

2 tbsp grated Parmesan

1   Wash the spinach leaves, shake them dry, and then pile them up on top of each other. Roll them up and slice into very fine ribbons.

2   Stir the spinach leaves and the Parmesan into the eggs along with the butter once you take the pan off the heat.

Eggcellent!

An egg is a meal in itself – boiled, poached, scrambled, baked, in an omelet and it's amazingly useful when it comes to all sorts of other recipes too.

Plenty of animals lay them but when we see egg in a recipe we just know that we're talking about hens. Thousands of years ago humans discovered how good these wild Asian jungle fowl were at laying loads of eggs and we've been breeding them ever since. Today there are almost 5 billion egg-laying hens in the world! Duck, goose, and quail eggs are tasty options too.

> It's no surprise that eggs are really packed with goodies – everything the chick needs to develop is inside that shell.

What happens if you play table tennis with a bad egg?

It goes ping, then it goes pong.

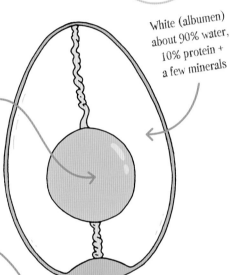

White (albumen) about 90% water, 10% protein + a few minerals

Yolk about 50% water, 20% protein, 30% fat + loads of vitamins and minerals

Cooks use eggs...

AS VARNISH
Brush pastries and breads with beaten egg to give them a glossy finish.

FOR THICKENING
Creamy rich yolks go into custards, sauces, and mayonnaise.

FOR CREATING TINY AIR BUBBLES
Egg whites are whisked for meringues, mousses, and soufflés, and whole eggs are beaten for cakes. The air bubbles make food springy and light.

FOR FIRMING AND SETTING
When eggs cook they become firm, trapping air in cakes and holding together a quiche or an omelet.

AS GLUE
Seal pastry, make burgers bind together, create batters, and stick on crispy breadcrumb crusts.

Porridge

SERVES 4

Jumbo oats are the star ingredient in "proper" English porridge. They are rolled whole oat groats that give this British staple a thick and nubby texture.

A bowl of porridge in the morning will keep you fueled up with energy until lunchtime. If you can't find jumbo oats, use old-fashioned rolled oats instead.

1¾ cups (150 g) jumbo oats

1 cup (250 ml) milk, almond milk, or coconut milk

3 cups (750 ml) water

a pinch of salt

1. Put the oats, milk, water, and salt together in a deep saucepan.

2. Place the pan over high heat and stir with a wooden spoon. Be sure to hold the handle of the pan to steady it as you stir.

3. As soon as the porridge starts to bubble and boil turn the heat down to a simmer (that's just the odd shudder and bubble).

4. Keep stirring for about 7 minutes until the mixture thickens and the oat flakes have collapsed.

5. Once the porridge looks really creamy you're done. Now it's time for the real fun adding your flavorings…

7 Days 7 Ways

Fruity and Nutty

Stir 1 grated apple and a handful of blackberries into the porridge for the last minute or two of cooking. Top with a few more blackberries, 2 tablespoons toasted hazelnuts, and 2–3 tablespoons runny honey.

Porridge + sweetness + fruit/nuts = a delicious and healthy start to the day

Tropical

Top the porridge with 2 sliced bananas, zest of 1 lime, and 2–3 tablespoons light brown sugar (this one is awesome if you use coconut milk in the porridge).

Pure Purple

Stir a handful of blueberries into the porridge pan right at the beginning with the oats. Make the porridge as usual. Stir 2 teaspoons of vanilla extract into the porridge once it is ready. Serve topped with another handful of blueberries and 2–3 tablespoons maple syrup.

Mediterranean

Top the porridge with 8 tablespoons Greek yogurt, 10 chopped up dried apricots, a good handful of raspberries, a handful of toasted flaked almonds or pistachios, and 4 tablespoons runny honey.

Crunchy

Sprinkle a handful of granola on top of each bowl and sweeten with about 2 tablespoons honey.

WHAAAAT!?

Crispy Bacon and Maple Syrup

Oh yes, this classic breakfast mix is just the best on porridge. Chop up 8 slices of cooked, crispy bacon and sprinkle over the cooked porridge. Sweeten with a swirl of maple syrup.

Chocolate Heaven

Stir 2 tablespoons cocoa powder into the porridge in the pan once it is ready. Sweeten with about 3 tablespoons light brown sugar. Sprinkle with 2 sliced bananas, a few raspberries, and some toasted sliced almonds, if you like.

Classic Pancakes

Serve with bacon and maple syrup or a fruit salad with honey and yogurt.

SOMETIMES CALLED SCOTCH PANCAKES OR DROP SCONES

These are very simple to make and such a treat for breakfast or brunch. Why not make this a Sunday morning ritual with a different version each week?

1 cup (125 g) self-rising white flour or self-rising whole-wheat flour or a mixture of both

a pinch of salt

1 medium egg

1 cup (250 ml) milk

4 tsp butter

1. Put the flour and salt into a large bowl and make a well in the middle.

2. Add the egg and milk and whisk everything together until just combined. Don't worry about a few lumps, overwhisking will make your pancakes tough.

3. Add a teaspoon of butter to a large frying pan and set the pan over high heat. Once the butter has melted, carefully add spoonfuls of pancake batter to the pan. You can cook them 4 or 5 at a time.

4. Once the tops of the pancakes are bubbly and the sides begin to firm, turn them over using a spatula (or two).

5. Cook for another minute or two, or until golden, and then place on a warm plate. They are scrumptious eaten straightaway, but you can cover them with foil to keep warm until you have used all the mixture.

6. Add another teaspoon of butter to the pan, let it melt, and spoon in your next batch of pancakes.

If the pan begins to smoke, turn the heat down.

④

Yummy with sugar and a squeeze of lemon juice.

Fruity Pancakes

Add 1 grated apple or pear (peel and all) to the pancake batter when you stir it all together.

OR

Add blueberries, raspberries, strawberries, or blackberries to the pancakes as soon as you have spooned the mixture into the pan. About 4 or 5 berries per pancake is plenty. Serve with honey.

OR

Stir 1 mashed banana and the grated zest of 1 lime into the pancake mix and serve sprinkled with toasted coconut chips, light brown sugar, and lime juice.

Go Savory

Stir ½ cup (50 g) grated Cheddar cheese into the batter with a tablespoon of chopped chives.

OR

Stir 1 generous cup (100 g) corn kernels and 2 chopped up green onions into the batter. So good served with a dollop of guacamole!

OR

Make the pancake batter with whole-wheat flour, 1 tablespoon chives, and chopped dill. Serve with smoked salmon and a blob of sour cream.

SMOOTHIES

Very Berry Smoothie

Pretty much any ripe fruit will make a delicious smoothie. Your smoothie should be a blend of liquid and fruit – half and half works well, so…

½ cup (100 ml) liquid +
a small handful of chopped fruit (100 g)
= 1 medium smoothie

Your liquid could be milk, almond milk, soy milk, rice milk, oat milk, coconut water, or orange or apple juice.

The method is simple:
Pop all the ingredients in the blender.
Blitz.
Hey presto, it's ready.

You'll need a blender to make these delicious fruit drinks – just watch those razor-sharp blades !!! and REMEMBER to cover with the lid before switching on, or you might redecorate the ceiling.

Remember to use and freeze berries when they are in season, as they usually taste better and will be cheaper too. It's fun collecting bags of blackberries in the autumn to use through the cold winter months when your body needs a vitamin boost.

12 oz (350 g) mixed berries – strawberries, raspberries, blueberries, blackberries

1 banana

1¾ cups (400 ml) chilled milk or apple juice

1 Slice the strawberries, break up the banana, and pop into the blender with the other fruit.

2 Pour in the milk or juice.

3 Put the lid on the blender tightly.

4 Blitz. That's it!

If your smoothie needs sweetening, add a little honey, maple syrup, or sugar.

More smoothie recipes → → →

Smoothie Tips

Leave apple/pear peel on –
it's full of goodness.

Add a couple of ice cubes to the
blender if you like drinks chilled.

Frozen fruit will make instant chilled
smoothies. Seasonal fruit from the market
or from an overflowing fruit bowl is great
to freeze – just cut it into chunks first.
You can get bags of frozen berries
at the supermarket too.

Bananas supply a lovely creamy texture,
but you can always add some
plain yogurt instead.

Green Super Smoothie

There's nothing to stop you from adding leafy vegetables for an extra vitamin hit. You won't taste the spinach leaves, but they'll give your smoothie the wow factor.

1¾ cups (400 ml) chilled almond milk, coconut water, or apple juice

2 bananas

1 apple – skin on

1 pear – skin on

a big handful of baby spinach leaves

juice of ½–1 lime

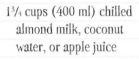

1 Put the liquid in the blender first, and add the chunks of fruit and leaves next. Add half the lime juice and whizz.

2 Taste. You can add more lime juice to the mix if you want to.

Get creative

How about a few mint or basil leaves or a teaspoon of grated ginger?

Ice pops

Smoothie mixes make delicious ice pops. You can pick up simple molds in most supermarkets during the summer months.

Once frozen, transfer the popsicles to well-sealed freezer bags, so that you can build up a selection.

You may want to give your smoothies a little extra sweetness with honey, maple syrup, or sugar because the cold will numb your taste buds.

Mango Lassi

MAKES 4

Here's a classic from North India, where everyone looks forward to the spring mango season and enjoys the fabulously sweet fruit in this refreshing drink.

A *lassi* doesn't actually have to have any fruit in it at all – it's really just a chilled yogurt drink, sometimes seasoned with salt!

2 ripe medium mangoes
(about 10¹⁄₂ oz/300 g flesh)

generous 1 cup (250 ml)
plain yogurt

5–6 ice cubes

1 tbsp honey, or to taste

splash of milk or water,
if you need it

1 Cut up your mangoes.

2 Put the fruit into the blender with the yogurt, ice cubes, and half of the honey.

3 Blend the fruit until smooth and then taste. You may need a bit more honey but the drink doesn't need to be too sweet.

4 If the lassi seems very thick, just add a splash of milk or water.

Go to p. 146 if you're not sure how.

Spice It Up

You could give your lassi some authentic Indian spicing with 2 cardamom pods.

Crack open the pods with a pestle and mortar, remove the outer husk, and grind the tiny black seeds. Throw these in with the rest of the ingredients before you blend them.

Go Nuts!

Sprinkle the top of the lassi with some chopped almonds or pistachios for a bit of crunch.

Cheat?

You can sometimes buy cans or packets of mango pulp, which work really well. If the mango pulp already has sugar added, then leave out the honey in your lassi.

No pestle and mortar? You can always use the end of a rolling pin in a heavy-duty bowl.

Cool
Stuff
picnics and packed lunches

RAW SLAWS

Great for tomorrow's lunchbox or picnic; delicious with a baked potato; fab rolled up in a wrap.

A slaw is a grated fruit or veggie salad. Here's your chance to "eat a rainbow" on one plate. You can decide which fruit and vegetables to include, so try to choose at least one from each color group — your salad won't just look and taste fabulous, it will be loaded with all sorts of different minerals and vitamins, keeping you healthy and full of energy.

The Basic Slaw

SERVES 4

2 green onions

2 carrots

2 small beets (1 red, 1 yellow if possible)

¼ head green cabbage

1 apple

a handful of raisins

DRESSING

juice of ½ lemon

3 tbsp extra-virgin olive oil

salt and pepper

OR one of the dressings on p. 41

1. Wash all the fresh vegetables and fruit really well. You'll need to give the root vegetables a good scrub because we want to eat the skin (it's chockablock with nutrients and fiber).

2. Chop the root from the green onions and peel off the outer skin, trim any ragged green tips, and slice the onion into thin rounds. Set aside.

3. Chop the tops off the carrots and beets but leave the peel on. Place a box grater on a chopping board and carefully grate the vegetables. Always stop well before your fingers meet the grater — you can chop up any leftover chunks with a knife.

4. Grate or finely slice the cabbage; the core will hold it together as you work, but you can throw this away later (rabbits and guinea pigs love these bits).

5 Chop the apple in half and remove the core. Grate the fruit, skin and all.

6 Put everything into a large bowl and add the raisins.

7 Add the lemon juice, olive oil, a pinch of salt, and a grind of pepper to the salad at once, before the apple begins to turn brown. Toss and turn everything carefully to mix in the dressing.

How about topping with some crunchy or sprouty sprinkles? (see p. 42)

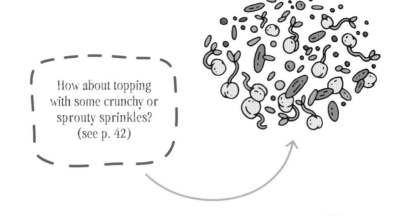

Here's another tasty slaw mix

SERVES 4

2 green onions

2 carrots

1/4 head red cabbage

8 radishes, grated or sliced

1/2 bulb of fennel; remove the tough outer layer and stalk before grating

1 pear

a handful seedless green grapes

DRESSING

juice of 1/2 lemon

3 tbsp extra-virgin olive oil

OR one of the dressings on p. 41

Follow the basic slaw method on the opposite page. You are just swapping the fruit and vegetables around.

That's the idea: mixing and matching depending on what's in season, what you love to eat, and what you might find in the fridge or the fruit bowl.

The world record for the fastest vegetable to run a marathon is held by Edward Lumley, who dressed as a carrot in the 2012 London Marathon. His time of 2 hours, 59 minutes, 33 seconds was helped by a last minute spurt when he heard that a runner bean was coming up behind. True story!

Summer Leafy Salads

SERVES 4

SALAD MATH

salad +
dressing +
sprinkly bits
=
lunch

There's no rule that says that you can't eat these in winter, but it's wise to eat vegetables when they are in season. They are usually fresher, tastier, and often much cheaper too. Wash all salad ingredients before using.

7 oz (200 g) lettuce leaves, washed

½ cucumber

12 cherry tomatoes

Choose a dressing from opposite

1 Dry your salad leaves in a salad spinner or with a few sheets of paper towel in a colander.

2 Slice or dice the cucumber and cut the cherry tomatoes in half.

3 Put your salad ingredients in a serving bowl and, once you're almost ready to eat, add 2 tablespoons of dressing. Now, with VERY clean hands or with salad servers, toss the salad gently to cover in the dressing. You may like to use a little more dressing, but it's always better to add dressings, sauces, and seasonings slowly, tasting as you go.

Add the dressing just a few minutes before serving or you'll end up with slimy lettuce →

EXTRAS

Maybe 2 of the following:

2 slices ham, chopped up

leftover chicken from a roast, chopped up

6 slices of smoked bacon, fried until crisp and then chopped up

chunks of avocado (toss in the dressing at once or it will go brown)

chunks of feta, goat's cheese, Cheddar, or blue cheese

a handful of toasted nuts, such as almonds, walnuts, or hazelnuts

3 Great Salad Dressings

Just put all the ingredients in a jar, close the lid TIGHTLY, and shake away.

Lemony Dressing

4 tbsp extra-virgin olive oil

juice of ½ lemon

1 tsp grainy mustard

a pinch of salt and a grind of pepper

optional extra – a few finely chopped leaves of an herb, such as basil, mint, parsley, or tarragon

Tahini Dressing

3 tbsp tahini

2 tbsp extra-virgin olive oil

juice of ½ orange

1 tbsp cider vinegar

a pinch of salt and a grind of black pepper

People often think that dressing is bad for you, but the good news is that we do all need a little bit of fat (from the oil) to help us absorb the minerals and vitamins in the salad.

Yogurt Dressing

4 tbsp plain yogurt

2 tbsp white wine vinegar

2 tbsp extra-virgin olive oil

a pinch of salt and a grind of pepper

optional extra – a few finely chopped leaves of an herb, such as basil, mint, parsley, or tarragon

Sprinkly Bits

Crunchy Sprinkles

It's good to make up a little jar of roasted nuts and seeds to throw into sandwiches, onto salads, and even over steamed vegetables, such as green beans or broccoli.

2 tbsp pumpkin seeds
2 tbsp sunflower seeds
2 tbsp sesame seeds
2 tbsp pine nuts

or hazelnuts, walnuts, or almonds – you're the boss

Put everything in a dry frying pan and place over medium heat. Stir for 2 or 3 minutes until the seeds and kernels begin to smell nutty. Pour them onto a large cold plate to cool and then store in a jar.

no, not brussels sprouts!

Sprouty Sprinkles

Plenty of health food shops and markets sell bags of sprouted lentils, beans, and chickpeas. Give them a try. Not just for the fact that they have a lovely nutty taste and crisp bite to them, but because they are PACKED with goodness too.

If you're not great at eating salads, these sprinkles are sure to get you started. Try some with a fruit or vegetable like apple or carrot to begin with or sprinkle some into a cheese or ham sandwich.

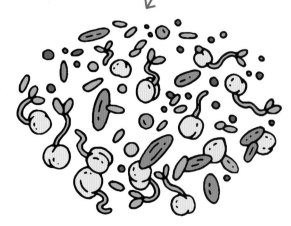

Croutons

Croutons are often fried, but these crunchy, toasty sprinkles are baked in the oven, which is easier and better for you too. They're great things to add to soups and salads. They will keep well in an airtight container for a week.

9 oz (250 g) bread (whole-wheat and sourdough breads make great croutons)

5 tbsp extra-virgin olive oil

$1/2$ tsp salt

optional – 2 tsp herbs, such as rosemary, thyme, or sage (dried or fresh, very finely chopped)

MAKES A LARGE BAGFUL

French for "crispy bread cubes"

1 Preheat the oven to 375°F (190°C).

2 Tear the bread into pieces the size of large dice, and place them on a baking sheet just one layer deep. Sprinkle over the olive oil and the salt.

3 Toss everything around with your hands until the bread has soaked up the oil. You may need to spread some of the bread onto a second tray if the bread is tightly packed. The pieces shouldn't touch each other, otherwise they won't crisp up.

4 Bake in the oven for 5 minutes. Remove from the oven and turn the croutons over with a spoon or spatula. If you are adding herbs, now's the time to sprinkle some in.

5 Place the croutons back in the oven for another 5 minutes, or until they are crisp and golden.

6 Carefully spoon or tip the croutons onto a wire rack to cool completely. Store in an airtight container or bag if you are not using them straightaway.

Super-speedy Bean and Tuna Salad

Here's a quick-and-easy salad that proves that canned food can be a healthy and very tasty option. You can choose which beans to use, such as borlotti, cannellini, pinto, or black beans.

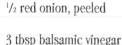

SERVES 4 AS A SIDE DISH WITH A BAKED POTATO OR 2 AS A MAIN COURSE

½ red onion, peeled

3 tbsp balsamic vinegar

1 x 14-oz (400-g) can beans in water

1 x 7-oz (200-g) can corn

1 x 7-oz (200-g) can tuna in olive oil

a small bunch of flat-leaf parsley

4 tbsp extra-virgin olive oil

a good pinch of salt and a grind of black pepper

1. Slice the red onion as finely as possible and then put it into your salad bowl with the vinegar.

2. Pour the beans into a colander over the sink and rinse them in some cold water. Shake off the excess water and pour them into the salad bowl.

3. Use the same colander to drain the corn and then the tuna, then put them in the salad bowl too.

4. Pinch the parsley leaves off the stalks and chop them roughly.

5. Now add the parsley, olive oil, salt, and pepper to the salad bowl. Take a spoon, mix everything well and then have a taste. Does the salad need more seasoning? Try to balance the oil, vinegar, salt, and pepper before you serve.

Great for the lunchbox because beans are packed with fiber, which keeps you feeling full and energetic for hours.

Do your bit for our oceans and buy tuna with a "dolphin-friendly" or "pole-and-line caught" label on the can.

Mexican Beans

Leave out the tuna, corn, and parsley and add 3 chopped tomatoes, 1 chopped avocado (see p. 51), a handful of cilantro leaves, and the juice of 1 lime.

Spanish Beans

Leave out the tuna and corn and add 3 chopped tomatoes and a handful of chopped chorizo (the hard, fully cured kind from the deli counter, not the soft stuff which still needs cooking).

Veggie Beans

Out with the tuna and corn and in with 3 chopped tomatoes, a handful of crumbled feta cheese, and a big handful of torn basil leaves. Eat this salad with a slice of bread and you've got a balanced vegetarian meal.

Super Seeds

It's no wonder that a seed is packed with goodness — it contains everything needed to burst into life as a new plant.

Cereal grains are the dry seeds from grassy plants. We produce about 2,500,000,000 tons of them every year — oh yes, that's a lot of zeros! The most widely grown are corn, rice, and wheat.

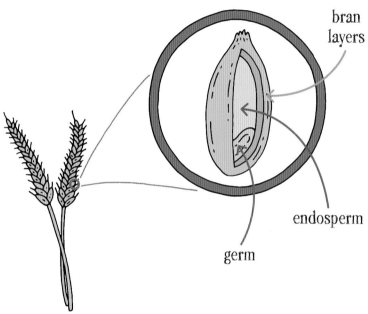

bran layers

endosperm

germ

Whole-grain foods such as brown rice or whole-wheat bread include the bran, the germ, and the endosperm. The bran gives us fiber, which takes a while for our bodies to digest so that we feel full and energized for longer. The germ is in fact the baby plant and is packed with healthy oil and lots of other nutrients.

White rice, and the white flour milled (ground) from wheat for pasta, cakes, and most of our bread, comes from the pale bit of the picture – the endosperm. This bit of the grain can give us plenty of energy, but it's a great shame to throw out the bran and the germ.

Always check before serving nuts to friends or taking them to school. Some people have very bad allergic reactions.

Pulses are seeds too — they just come in pods

The good news is, whether you buy them dried or ready cooked, chickpeas, lentils, peas, and beans are "whole foods." That means we eat them just as they are, without getting rid of any of the good parts.

Making your own baked beans or hummus is cheap, easy, fun, and scrumptious.

Throwing a few pulses into a salad makes it more filling and will keep you fueled up with energy for hours.

OK, there's the wind factor too. That's the helpful bacteria in your intestines creating gas while they help you break down the good-for-you fiber. (It's always handy to have a pet or a baby in the family to blame it on!) If it really is a problem, try cooking ginger, turmeric, cumin, or a small piece of dried kombu seaweed with your beans.

Nuts and Other Seeds

Nuts are seeds that we find in a shell. Other tasty seeds come from flowers, pods, or fruits. They make really healthy snacks, especially if you eat them by the handful instead of in a "health bar" where they are held together with loads of sticky sugar. Try sprinkling nuts and seeds over salads and into sandwiches.

Nuts contain healthy fats. We need good fat to give us energy, make our brains and nerves work well, carry vitamins around our bloodstream, give us healthy skin, and loads of other stuff.

Preparing Grains

! ! !
Boiling water alert!!!

How to Prepare Bulgur Wheat

Put ½ cup (100 g) bulgur wheat in a large bowl and pour over generous ¾ cup (200 ml) of boiling water.

Cover with plastic wrap and leave for 20 minutes. Pour the bulgur wheat into a sieve to drain any excess water and put into a bowl.

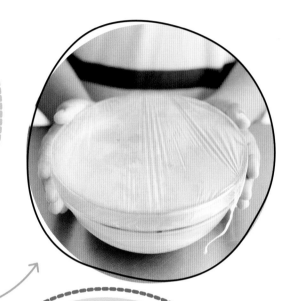

How to Prepare Quinoa

Rinse ⅔ cup (100 g) quinoa in a sieve before cooking to get rid of any bitter taste.

Put the quinoa in a saucepan with generous ¾ cup (200 ml) cold water and bring it up to a boil. Turn the heat down to a low simmer (just the odd bubble) and cook for about 15 minutes.

You can tell when quinoa is cooked because each little seed develops a halo around it. Pour the quinoa into a sieve to drain away excess water.

This is one brainy plant — the bitter flavor, called saponin, which is on the outside of the seeds, stops insects from eating them.

47

Mediterranean Bulgur Salad

SERVES 4

Bulgur wheat is a favorite in Eastern Mediterranean countries. It's cracked whole wheat, so it's packed with goodness and is really quick to prepare too.

½ cup (100 g) bulgur wheat

4 tomatoes

½ medium cucumber

2 green onions

2 sprigs of mint

4 sprigs of flat-leaf parsley

juice of ½–1 lemon

4 tbsp extra-virgin olive oil

salt

1 Prepare your bulgur wheat (see p. 47).

2 Chop the tomatoes and cucumber, seeds and all, into small chunks.

3 Chop the root from the green onions and peel off the outer skin, trim any ragged green leaf tips and slice. Pull the leaves off the herb stalks and chop or rip them roughly.

4 Mix the tomatoes, cucumber, green onions, and herbs with the bulgur wheat.

5 Pour over the lemon juice, olive oil, and a good pinch of salt.

THESE SALADS ARE GREAT FOR LUNCHBOXES, PICNICS, OR AS SIDE SALADS WITH BARBECUED MEATS AND FISH.

TRY crumbling 7 oz (200 g) feta cheese over the salad for a great lunch dish.

TRY adding cubes of watermelon instead of the tomato.

You can mix and match these salad recipes with any of the grains or seeds like bulgur wheat, couscous, or quinoa.

South American Quinoa Salad

SERVES 4

Adding grains and seeds to a salad makes it more filling and gives you the vital carbohydrates that you need for energy. Quinoa seeds come from the high plains of the Andes, in South America. Quinoa is often known as a "superfood" because it's packed with nutrients and protein, which makes it great for vegetarians.

²/₃ cup (100 g) quinoa

2 limes

1 avocado

1 red bell pepper

2 green onions

a small bunch cilantro

a handful of roasted cashew nuts

4 tbsp extra-virgin olive oil or cold-pressed canola oil

salt and pepper

1 Prepare your quinoa (see p. 47).

2 Grate the zest from half a lime and then squeeze all the juice from both limes into a small bowl.

3 Prepare your avocado.

4 Drop the avocado pieces into the lime juice and tumble them around straightaway so that they don't go brown.

5 Cut the red pepper in half and pull out the core, seeds, and stalk, then cut the flesh into small squares. Peel off the outer skin of the green onions and slice into thin rounds, throwing out the root, and pull the leaves from the cilantro stalks.

6 Pour the cooked quinoa into a bowl and allow to cool for a few minutes before throwing in the avocado and lime juice, the onions, pepper, cashew nuts, cilantro, and oil. Sprinkle with a good pinch of salt and some black pepper.

7 Take a large spoon and mix very carefully so that the avocado does not get too squashed and mushy. Have a taste; do you need more salt or pepper?

(7)

TRY adding cold chicken to the salad.

TRY adding a pinch of cayenne pepper or some very finely chopped chile if you like some HEAT!!!

How to Prepare Avocado

Cut the avocado in half with a small knife – you will meet the pit in the middle; don't try to cut through it! Just twist the halves apart. Cut the flesh inside each half in a grid pattern (without going through the skin), then just scoop the cubes out with a spoon.

(3)

51

Guacamole

SERVES 4

Homemade guacamole is an absolute treat. You can eat it as a dip with potato or pita chips, and it can also be fab with a baked potato (p. 118), a bowl of designer baked beans (p. 85), or some chili con carne (p. 114).

2 green onions, trimmed and finely sliced

1–2 chiles, diced very finely (check the heat)

juice of 1 lime

2–3 RIPE avocados

2 medium tomatoes, diced

a handful of cilantro leaves, roughly chopped

salt and pepper

1 Put the green onions and half of the chiles in a bowl and pour over the lime juice.

2 Now peel and roughly chop the avocados before adding them to the bowl and mashing roughly with the back of a fork.

3 Stir in the tomatoes, most of the cilantro, and add some salt and pepper.

4 Taste. Add more chile, salt, and pepper if you think your guacamole needs more attitude.

Don't like cilantro? Leave it out, amigo!

Need a reminder on chopping avocado? Go to p. 51.

Hummus

SERVES 4

HUMMUS IS THE ARABIC WORD FOR CHICKPEAS

Hummus takes minutes to make if you have a food processor or blender.
It's just a question of whizzing everything together.

1 x 14-oz can (400 g) chickpeas
juice of 2 lemons
2 garlic cloves, peeled and crushed
4–6 tbsp tahini (sesame seed paste – you can find it in the supermarket)
2 tbsp water
salt and black pepper or cayenne pepper
2 tbsp extra-virgin olive oil
1 tsp paprika
1 tbsp chopped parsley

1 Pour the chickpeas into a colander and rinse them under the faucet.

2 Put the chickpeas in a food processor with the lemon juice and garlic. Give the tahini a good stir and then add 4 tablespoons along with the water.

3 Blend until the mixture is really smooth, then add more water to thin it down if necessary. Taste and season with a good pinch of salt.

4 Serve in a small bowl drizzled with the extra-virgin olive oil and sprinkled with the paprika and parsley. Or you could spoon the hummus into a container and keep it in the fridge for a couple of days for sandwiches or dipping vegetables.

Spice it up

Try adding 2 teaspoons ground cumin or a good pinch of cayenne pepper.

Different but just as good

It might not be traditional Middle Eastern hummus, but you can leave out the tahini and add ⅔ cup (150 ml) extra-virgin olive oil instead.

PITA

Pita bread makes an ideal edible container for all sorts of slaws and lettuce or bean salads. Just cut the pita in half, then open it up like a pocket and stuff everything inside. Add a spoonful of hummus (see p. 54) or creamy guacamole (see p. 52), and you've got an instant packed lunch, picnic, or simple meal.

Pita Chips

 SERVES 4

4 pita breads
extra-virgin olive oil
salt
dried herbs or spices (optional)

1 Preheat the oven to 325°F (160°C).

2 Cut the pitas into 1-in (2.5-cm) strips with a pair of scissors. Separate the "loops" of bread into single strips.

3 Place the pita strips on baking sheets. There always seem to be thinner and thicker sides to the bread, so have a tray of quicker-cooking, more delicate chips and another tray for the thicker pieces.

4 Drizzle over a few drops of extra-virgin olive oil and season with a little salt. You can add dried herbs or spices at this point too.

5 Toss the bread around to cover in the seasoning and arrange in a single layer.

6 Place in the oven until dried out and crisp, about 10–20 minutes. You'll have to keep an eye on them so they don't burn.

7 Cool on a wire rack and then store the chips in an airtight container until ready to use. They will keep their crunch for a couple of weeks.

A HEALTHY BUT SCRUMPTIOUS ALTERNATIVE TO POTATO CHIPS

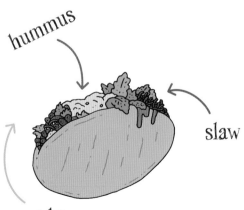

hummus

slaw

sprinkly seeds

FLATBREADS AND WRAPS

Try rolling up any of the leafy or bean salads or the crunchy slaws and add some cream cheese, grated cheese, hummus, or guacamole.

OR go Mexican with chili con carne, guacamole, and sour cream.

1 Place your filling in the lower two-thirds of your bread.
2 Tuck in the sides.
3 Roll up.

Simple as that – it's a wrap!

Bowl
Food

dishes to spoon and slurp

Real Chicken Stock

MAKES 4 CUPS (1 LITER)

Next time you enjoy a roast chicken (see p. 99), make sure that the bones don't get thrown away. Alternatively, you could see if your butcher has some carcasses to spare. This stock will make your soups and sauces taste amazing and can also be the star player in a simple broth.

bones from at least 1 chicken, raw or cooked

1 onion, sliced in half

1 dried bay leaf

1 tsp black peppercorns

2 tbsp cider vinegar

1　Put all the ingredients into a large saucepan and pour in 6 cups (1.5 liters) cold water to cover the bones by about 4 inches (10 cm). Check the liquid level about once every 30 minutes and top up with water to cover the bones if needed.

2　Place the pan over high heat and bring it to a boil. Use a spoon to skim off the fatty froth that rises to the top of the pan, then turn the heat really low, cover with a lid, and leave for at least a couple of hours or, better still, 5 or 6 hours.

3　Strain the stock through a fine-mesh sieve and it's ready to use.

It's a great idea to freeze some stock in small containers so that you've always got some on hand. It keeps for up to 6 months.

Long, gentle cooking of your stock breaks down the bones and gives you a super-duperly nutritious liquid packed with protein, minerals, and collagen. Chicken noodle soup is often considered a major pick-me-up if you've got the flu or a cold.

NO, WE'RE NOT TALKING FAST FOOD IN A POT!

OODLES OF NOODLES

Asian noodles are really quick and easy to prepare. There are dozens of types to choose from. Some are ready cooked and can be stirred into a soup or stir-fry just as they are, but most types are dried.

Noodle Know-how

Allow 3½ oz (100 g) of dried noodles per person.

If you use a big pot to boil the noodles they won't stick together. You should allow 4 cups (1 liter) water for each 3½ oz (100 g) noodles.

Asian-style noodles often contain salt already, so check the package before adding salt to the water.

Allow the water to boil before adding the noodles.

Always check to see if the noodles are cooked a minute earlier than it says on the package.

Pour into a colander in the sink to drain — beware of the hot steam as well as the water.

super-healthy

Japanese soba noodles

are made with buckwheat flour. They are whole grain, taste nutty, and are really filling. Eat them hot or cold.

Great added to a stir-fry at the last moment

Chinese egg noodles and Japanese ramen

are made with wheat flour, eggs, and salt. Take care not to overcook them — some of the thin varieties take just a minute. They should seem springy rather than sloppy when they're ready.

White wheat noodles

are made from wheat, salt, and water.

Japanese udon noodles

are quite thick and chewy. The tough dough is traditionally kneaded using your feet!

Rice noodles

are made from rice. You can get thick ribbons or fine "angel hair." They DON'T need to be cooked, just soaked in boiling water until they have softened, then strained and a teaspoon of vegetable oil added if you are not cooking them right away.

Cellophane or glass noodles

may look like cellophane or glass when cooked, but are in fact made from mung beans or yam or potato starch. Just add boiling water until they've softened and then strain. Awesome in cold salads.

CHINESE EGG NOODLES

In Japan they eat soba noodles at New Year's, as long noodles promise long life... so don't break them!

RICE NOODLES

JAPANESE SOBA NOODLES

Try with chopped cucumber, fresh mint or cilantro leaves, cold cooked prawns, and roasted peanuts. Make a dressing with grated ginger, lime juice, and soy sauce. Yum!

JAPANESE UDON NOODLES

Noodles are great with marinated salmon, chicken skewers, Vietnamese meatballs, a stir-fry, or just some steamed vegetables with chopped green onions and a dash of soy sauce.

Chicken Noodle Bowl

SERVES 4

1 tsp grated fresh ginger

1 garlic clove, peeled and crushed

1 stalk of lemongrass

5 cups (1.2 liters) chicken stock (see p. 60)

3½ oz (100 g) noodles

1–2 tbsp soy sauce — (see p. 62)

3 green onions, trimmed and finely chopped

a few cilantro or basil leaves

1–2 chiles, very finely sliced (optional)

1 lime, cut into quarters

Check out the heat
OR
serve with sweet chile sauce at the table

1. Prepare the ginger and garlic. Then chop the tip off the lemongrass and remove the tough outer layer before slicing it finely.

2. Heat up the stock in a large saucepan with the ginger, garlic, and lemongrass. Once the stock is boiling add your noodles and cook until they're ready.

3. Season the broth with soy sauce and sprinkle with the green onions and a few leaves of cilantro or basil. Add a little chile, if using, and serve with a wedge of lime.

Some noodles only take a minute or two, so do look at the package instructions.

Spice It Up

by adding bean sprouts, snow peas, or thin slices of red pepper or carrot for a minute of cooking before serving.

Try

shredding any leftover chicken from a roast and adding it to the broth for a couple of minutes, just to heat through.

Corn Chowder

 **SERVES 4**

Watch out! You might not need much because the bacon is salty.

There are all sorts of different chowder recipes, but you only really need one. Learn to cook the simple chowder here, then you can play around with all sorts of variations.

The potato makes this a filling dish, so you could serve this with some crusty bread for a great supper.

1 onion

3 slices of smoked bacon

3½ tbsp butter

1 lb (500 g) potatoes

1¼ cups (300 ml) vegetable stock or water

2 green onions, trimmed and finely sliced

2½ cups (600 ml) whole milk

1¼ cups (150 g) corn, canned or frozen

salt and pepper

4 tbsp heavy cream (optional)

a small handful of basil leaves

1 Cut the onion into small dice (see p. 13). Slice the bacon into tiny pieces.

2 Melt the butter in a large saucepan over a medium heat and add the onion and bacon. Cook for about 10 minutes until the onion is really soft.

3 Peel your potatoes and cut them into medium dice. Add the potatoes to the pan and cook, stirring, for about 5 minutes.

4 Pour in the vegetable stock or water and bring to a boil. Cook the potatoes until they are just tender (about 10 minutes). You can get your green onions sliced and ready for topping the soup while you are waiting.

5 Add the milk and corn and then simmer the soup over low heat for a couple of minutes.

6 Season with a pinch of salt and a grind of black pepper. Stir in the heavy cream. It's not absolutely necessary but does make the soup more of a treat.

7 Ladle the soup into bowls. Tear the basil leaves and scatter them over the soup along with the sliced green onions. Serve and wait for the applause.

Smoked Haddock Chowder

12 oz (350 g) skinned and boned smoked haddock fillet

Your most important job is to check the fish for bones. Run your fingers over the fish, especially in the center of the fillet and pull out any bones you find.

Cut the fish into 4 pieces.

Follow the recipe for Corn Chowder and add the fish to the soup at the same time as the milk and corn. You will be surprised by how little time it takes to cook.

The fish is ready as soon as the flesh is opaque (not transparent) and it begins to flake if you press it with a fork. Stop cooking and spoon out the soup, trying to keep some large chunky pieces of fish.

Sprinkle over the green onions and basil and serve piping hot.

Ask the fishmonger to do this for you.

Eat Your Veggies

We could all do with eating more vegetables. They really are the superheroes of the food world. They help us fight off disease, keep our digestive system and bloodstream healthy, strengthen our bones, are great for our eyes, and make our skin glow too. Vegetables also have plenty of fiber that fills us up, rather than fattening us up.

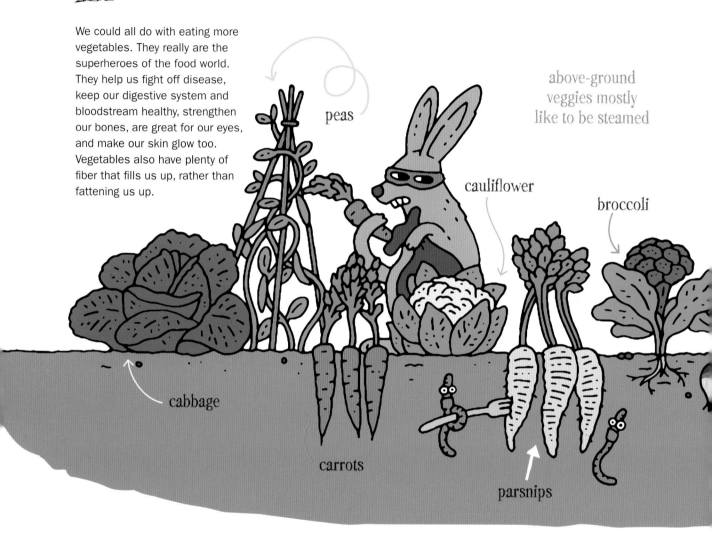

peas

above-ground veggies mostly like to be steamed

cauliflower

broccoli

cabbage

carrots

parsnips

below-ground veggies mostly like to be roasted

How to Roast Veggies

Root vegetables are especially tasty if you roast them — try any mixture of these in the picture. Cook plenty — they are scrumptious hot or cold. Try adding a sprig of rosemary and thyme to the roasting pan too.

How to Steam Veggies

Great as a side dish with a pinch of salt and pepper, and add a splash of olive oil or perhaps a little butter. OR fab as a simple supper with a dash of soy sauce and some rice or noodles.

Steaming is a great way to keep all the goodness in vegetables. Lots of nutrients and flavor are washed away in the water when you boil them.

You can buy electric steamers, but all you really need is a saucepan with a lid and a steamer basket, or a steamer pan that fits on your saucepan, or a bamboo steamer and a wok.

1 Wash and cut up the vegetables into bite-size slices, sticks, or ribbons (good for leafy veg).

2 Pour water into the pan underneath your steamer, put on the lid and place over high heat. Once the water is boiling you are ready to go.

3 Remove the lid using oven mitts. Remember, steam can burn!

4 Put the vegetables in the steamer and replace the lid. Steam for 5–10 minutes. Keep them a little bit crunchy — they will taste fantastic and be healthier too.

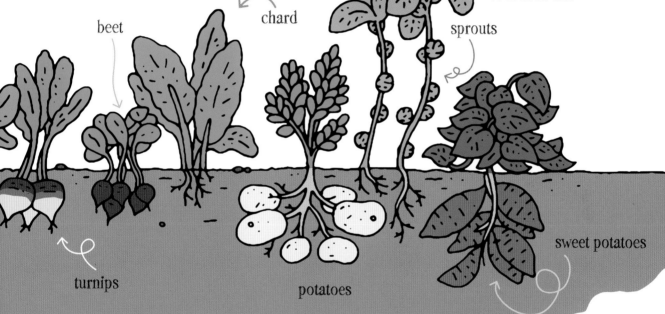

beet

chard

sprouts

turnips

potatoes

sweet potatoes

1 Preheat the oven to 400°F (200°C).

2 Wash and peel the vegetables and cut into rough 2-in (5-cm) chunks.

3 Put the veggies into a large roasting pan, not too crowded, just one layer deep.

4 Sprinkle with salt, pepper, and splash over about 2 tablespoons of olive oil. Roll the veggies around to coat them in oil.

5 Roast in the hot oven for about 45 minutes. Every 15 minutes, take the pan out and turn the vegetables over to cook evenly.

Eat as a side dish with a dash of balsamic vinegar. OR pile up on some brown rice and top with goat's cheese or yogurt OR try adding to a grain salad.

Minestrone

SERVES 4-6

Minestrone means "big soup" in Italian, and that's no exaggeration: with pasta, potatoes, and beans in it, this really is a meal in a bowl.

You can swap the veggies around with the seasons and make sure you include all your favorites. Try adding diced butternut squash instead of the potato.

---

2 tbsp olive oil

1 onion, diced

2 carrots, diced

2 stalks of celery, diced

4 cups (1 liter) vegetable or chicken stock

1 potato, peeled and diced into ¾-in (2-cm) pieces

salt and pepper

1 x 14-oz (400-g) can diced tomatoes

1 x 14-oz (400-g) can borlotti or cannellini beans, drained

a handful of tiny pasta shapes, such as stelle or broken-up spaghetti

about 10½ oz (300 g) of green veggies, trimmed and cut into bite-size pieces – try green beans, zucchini, asparagus, peas, snow peas, kale, cabbage...

---

1 Heat the oil in a large saucepan over low heat and add the onion, carrot, and celery. Cook for about 5 minutes until the onion is soft.

2 Add the stock to the pan along with the diced potato and a pinch of salt and simmer for a couple of minutes. ✳

3 Add the tomatoes, beans, and pasta carefully; you don't want to get splashed with searing hot liquid. Turn up the heat, give it a stir, and allow the soup to boil for about 5 minutes.

✳ not quite boiling, just the odd bubble

ON THE TOP

3 tbsp grated Parmesan cheese

about 20 torn basil leaves

OR

3 tbsp pesto

---

4 Now add the greens and bubble for a couple of minutes until the vegetables are just cooked through but still crisp and bright.

5 Taste. Season with salt and pepper if you think it needs it, but remember that your Parmesan will be salty too.

6 Sprinkle with Parmesan and basil leaves (or stir in your pesto) and ladle into bowls to serve.

7 Buon Appetito!

Enjoy!

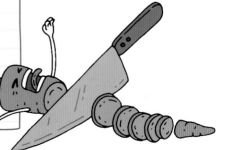

When you finish a chunk of Parmesan cheese keep the rind, as it's packed with flavor. Next time you are making minestrone add the rind, in one piece, with the stock then take out the soft, rubbery rind before serving.

Indian Lentil and Tomato Dal

SERVES 4–6 AS A MAIN OR 8–10 AS A SIDE DISH

Just add some extra water or stock and you've got a soup!

Dal is one of the cheapest and healthiest dishes you can ever make, and it's delicious too. You can eat it with boiled rice or flat, Indian-style breads, or as a side dish with a curry.

1¼ cups (250 g) red lentils

2½ cups (600 ml) water

2 medium onions, peeled and chopped

2 garlic cloves, peeled and crushed

1¼-in (3-cm) piece of fresh ginger, peeled and grated

3–4 tbsp vegetable oil, such as sunflower or canola oil

1 tsp ground turmeric

1 x 14-oz (400-g) can diced tomatoes

1 cup (200 ml) coconut milk

salt

FOR THE TARKA TOPPING

2 tbsp vegetable oil

1 tbsp black mustard seeds or cumin seeds and a pinch of red pepper flakes

a handful of chopped cilantro or mint leaves

1 Soak the lentils in the measured water while you prepare the onions, garlic, and ginger.

2 Add the vegetable oil to a large saucepan, place it over medium heat, then add the onions and sauté gently until they soften. Next, add the garlic and ginger and stir over the heat until the smell wafts up at you. Sprinkle in the turmeric and take the pan off the heat.

3 Now, carefully add the tomatoes, coconut milk, and the lentils with their water.

4 Put the pan back on the heat and simmer, or bubble, slowly, for about 20 minutes until the lentils have collapsed and you have a creamy mixture.

5 Taste the dal and add salt to balance the flavors.

6 To make the topping, take a small pan and warm the oil over medium heat, then add the seeds and fry for about a minute until they begin to pop.

7 Spoon the oil and seeds onto the dal. Stir and serve with a good sprinkling of chopped cilantro or mint.

Try

Using 2 x 14-oz (440-g) cans of chickpeas instead of the lentils. Just drain the chickpeas and add to the pan with the tomatoes and coconut milk. Cook for about 10 minutes and then add the tarka topping.

Give them
a stir every
5 minutes
or so.

Watch out,
they may
froth up
and spit!

Vegetable Stir-fry

SERVES 4

Our sense of taste varies, so have some soy sauce and sweet chile sauce on the table for everyone to season their food.

Frying vegetables in a wok is a fast and simple route to a healthy meal. Serve with brown or white rice or with noodles. Be sure to prepare all your ingredients before you begin cooking, as once you start frying everything will be ready quicker than you can say the words

That's Chinese for stir-fry!

炒菜

FOR THE BASE MIX

4 green onions, trimmed and finely sliced

¾-in (2-cm) piece of fresh ginger, peeled and very finely chopped

1 garlic clove, peeled and finely chopped

1 chile (optional), seeds removed if it is a hot one

FOR THE VEGGIES

1 red bell pepper, deseeded and cut into slices

2 carrots, cut into matchsticks or slices

1 medium zucchini, cut into matchsticks or slices

a handful of snow peas, tops trimmed

a handful of baby corn, sliced in half lengthwise

COOKING AND FINISHING OFF

2 tbsp vegetable oil

2 tbsp water

2 tbsp soy sauce

1 tbsp sesame seeds, for sprinkling

2 tbsp chopped cilantro (optional)

Swap these around with broccoli, bok choy, green beans, asparagus, or anything else you fancy.

1 Once you have chopped all your base mix ingredients put them into a bowl together. Place all your vegetables in another bowl, so that they are all ready to go.

2 Heat the oil in a wok or really large frying pan over high heat.

3 Add the base mix and stir over the high heat for 30 seconds; it will smell amazing.

4 Toss in the vegetables and stir over the heat for about 2 minutes. Add the water; be careful, as you'll have an impressive puff of steam. Stir for a couple of minutes longer until your vegetables are just cooked.

5 Take the wok off the heat and add the soy sauce.

6 Tip everything into a serving bowl and sprinkle over the sesame seeds and chopped cilantro, if using.

Try using a teaspoon to peel ginger.

Be sure to hold onto the wok handle while you stir this dish.

No longer or you will burn the garlic.

①

④

Shrimp and Vegetable Stir-fry

SERVES 4

You need raw, peeled shrimp for this dish. If they have been frozen, make sure that they are completely defrosted but are kept in the fridge until you are ready to use them.

I like to use all green veggies for this dish, such as asparagus, green beans, and zucchini, but it's up to you.

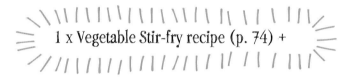

1 x Vegetable Stir-fry recipe (p. 74) +

7 oz (200 g) peeled raw large shrimp
grated zest and juice of 1 lime

1 Follow the Veggie Stir-fry recipe on p. 74.

2 Add the shrimp at the same time as the vegetables. Fry a little, and then add your water, and keep stirring until the shrimp are pink and opaque (not transparent).

3 Take the wok off the heat, add the soy sauce, sesame seeds, and cilantro (if using). Sprinkle with lime zest and squeeze over the lime juice just before serving.

Try

stirring some cooked noodles into the wok just before serving.

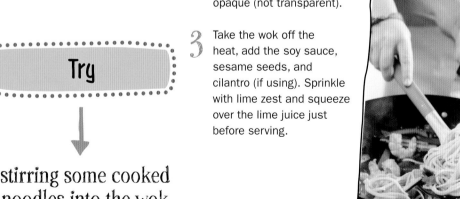

Egg-fried Rice with Stir-fried Veggies

SERVES 4

You will need a full-size wok for this recipe or cook it in two batches
(it's very quick in any case).

Need reminding?
go to
p. 80

1¼ cups (250 g) white rice
(see p. 80)

2 cups (500 ml) water

½ tsp salt

1 x Vegetable Stir-fry recipe
(p. 74)

2 eggs

2 tsp sesame oil

1 First, cook your rice. Rinse the rice in a sieve under the faucet. Boil the measured water and salt in a pan with a tight-fitting lid. Add the rice, put the lid on top, turn down the heat to really low, and cook for 15 minutes. Turn off the heat and leave the rice to cool while you prepare your vegetables.

2 Stir the eggs and sesame oil together in a mug with a fork.

3 Follow the vegetable stir-fry recipe and pour in the rice at the same time as the vegetables.

4 Once the rice and vegetables are ready, make a well in the middle of the wok and pour in the egg mixture. It will begin to set after about 10 seconds. Break it up with your spoon and stir into the rice and vegetables.

5 Add your soy sauce, sesame seeds, and cilantro from the vegetable stir-fry recipe and you are ready to serve.

ALMOST HALF OF THE WORLD'S 7 BILLION PEOPLE EAT RICE AS A MAINSTAY OF THEIR DAILY DIET.

Rather than weighing rice it's better to measure the volume – just remember 1 part rice to 2 parts water.

SERVES 4

How to Cook Brown Rice

Brown rice is a whole grain, so it includes all the bran and germ (see p. 46). It's chewy and has much more flavor than white rice.

2 cups brown rice

4 cups water

$^1/_2$ tsp salt

Rinse the rice in a sieve under the tap.

Boil the water and salt in a pan with a tight-fitting lid.

Add the rice to the pan and put the lid on. Once you can hear the water bubbling and boiling turn the heat down really low and cook for 25 minutes.

Now you can lift the lid and check whether the rice is cooked. It may need about 5–10 more minutes with the lid on. There should be some water left in the bottom of the pan (if not add 2 tablespoons).

Continue to cook over low heat until the rice is ready. It should be slightly chewy but soft in the middle. Turn off the heat and leave the rice to rest with the lid on for at least 5 minutes before serving. The rice should be soft and fluffy but not sticky.

How to Cook White Rice

White rice cooks quickly because the outer layers of bran have been removed, so it can become sticky and gluey if you add too much water. Follow this method and you'll get perfect fluffy rice every time.

2 cups long-grain rice

4 cups water

$^1/_2$ tsp salt

Rinse the rice in a sieve under the tap.

Boil the water and salt in a pan with a tight-fitting lid.

Add the rice to the pan and put the lid on. Once the water is boiling again (you can hear it bubbling), turn the heat down really low and cook for 15 minutes.

Turn off the heat and leave the rice to rest with the lid on for at least 5 minutes before serving.

Try with meatballs and tomato sauce or with chili con carne.

Just right with all sorts of stir-fries and curries.

PASTA

spaghetti, tagliatelle

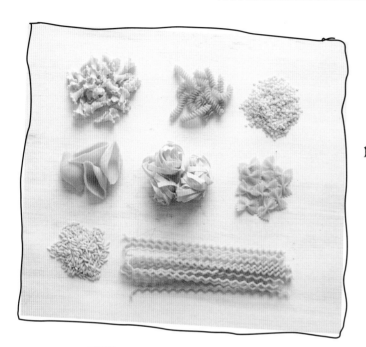

Italian pasta is traditionally made with durum wheat, and although it started its life as long ribbons, just like Asian noodles, nowadays you can buy literally hundreds of different shapes.

Pasta can be made with or without eggs and can be found fresh or dried, so check out the cooking times on the package.

How to Cook Pasta to Perfection

Allow 3½ oz (100 g) dried pasta per person.

Use a big pan and boil 4 cups (1 liter) water for every 3½ oz (100 g) pasta.

Salt the water and only add pasta to the water once it is boiling.

Don't overcook it; always check the pasta or noodles at least a minute before it says to on the package!!!! Take a piece of the pasta, allow to cool for a few seconds, and then taste. The pasta should still be a bit firm in the middle; the Italians like it with a bit of bite — what they call "al dente."

Drain in a colander in the sink, reserving a tiny bit of water in case you need to make your sauce a little thinner.

Serve with a homemade tomato sauce (see p. 82), ragù (see p. 110), pesto OR try this...

often called Bolognese sauce

Almost-Instant Fresh Tomato and Basil Sauce

SERVES 4

2 garlic cloves

4 tbsp extra-virgin olive oil

14 oz (400 g) cherry tomatoes

about 20 basil leaves

1 Peel the garlic cloves and cut them in half lengthwise.

2 Put the garlic into a large frying pan with the olive oil and place the pan over the lowest heat possible. You're not cooking the garlic, just flavoring the oil.

3 Cut the cherry tomatoes in half and add them to the warm pan. The gentle heat will soften the tomatoes and make them taste sweeter and more intense too.

4 Heat the pan for about 10 minutes then remove the garlic with a slotted spoon (its job is done).

5 Tear the basil leaves into pieces; it's not just about making them smaller — you release the flavor too.

6 Stir the sauce into the freshly drained pasta in a bowl and serve with freshly grated Parmesan cheese.

Tomato Sauce

SUPER-USEFUL SAUCE

SERVES 6-8

Great with pasta, meatballs, beans, enchiladas, and loads of other good stuff too.

You won't believe that anyone could ever buy tomato sauce in a jar after you've tried this.

This recipe makes quite a large quantity, so you can keep the sauce for up to five days in the fridge, or you can freeze it.

1 onion
2 tbsp olive oil
2 garlic cloves
2 x 14-oz (400-g) cans plum tomatoes
pinch of salt and a good grind of black pepper
1 tsp sugar

1 Peel and chop the onion into small dice.

2 Warm the oil in a large saucepan over low heat and then tip in the onions. Cook slowly for 10 minutes, stirring once in a while, until the onions become really soft but not browned.

3 Meanwhile, peel and chop the garlic cloves really finely.

4 Add the garlic to the onions and stir, over the heat, until you can really smell it.

That means barely a bubble

5 Tip in the tomatoes and add a pinch of salt, a twist of pepper and the sugar. Now leave the sauce over a very low heat to simmer, for about 30 minutes. Give the sauce a stir once in a while just to be sure that it is not catching and burning on the bottom of the pan.

6 Taste and add more salt, pepper, or sugar, just a little bit at a time, until your sauce is perfect.

Great with pasta

Soooo good with black beans

ITALIAN TOMATO SAUCE
Serves 6–8

1 x TOMATO SAUCE + 3 sprigs of basil

Just put the sprigs to simmer in the sauce with the tomatoes (you can fish them out once it is ready). Tear up the leaves and add them to the sauce just before serving.

MEXICAN TOMATO SAUCE
Serves 6–8

1 x TOMATO SAUCE +
1 tsp dried oregano
1 tsp ground cumin
1 tsp smoked paprika
(hot or sweet)

Stir the oregano and spices into the pan at the same time as the garlic. Once your kitchen smells like a Mexican cantina (after about a minute), you can pour in the tomatoes.

MOROCCAN TOMATO SAUCE
Serves 6–8

Very tasty with meatballs

1 x TOMATO SAUCE +
1 tsp ground cumin
1/2 tsp ground cinnamon
1 tsp paprika
(not the smoky one)
a handful of cilantro
leaves, roughly chopped

Add the cumin, cinnamon, and paprika at the same time as the garlic. Add plenty of roughly chopped cilantro leaves to serve.

DESIGNER BAKED BEANS

Serves 4 as a side dish, 2 as a main with bread

Use a half quantity of the Tomato Sauce recipe per can of drained beans. Cook for about 10 minutes to warm through. Here are some great combinations...

½ x Italian Sauce + 1 x 14-oz (400-g) can cannellini beans

½ x Mexican Sauce + 1 x 14-oz (400-g) can black beans

½ x Moroccan Sauce + 1 x 14-oz (400-g) can chickpeas

Hot Favorites

fancy dinners to simple suppers

Fishy Business

Fish and shellfish are not only delicious, they're incredibly good for you too. More than a billion people around the world depend on fish as their number one source of protein.

Fish are also packed with vitamins and minerals and are really simple to prepare. Try giving them the paper bag treatment on p. 90.

A portion of crispy, battered fish and chips is a real treat once in a while too.

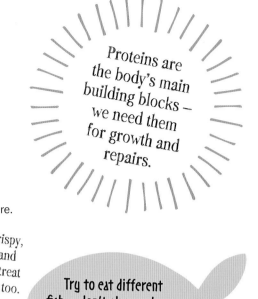

Proteins are the body's main building blocks – we need them for growth and repairs.

Which fish to eat?

Well, there are more than 25,000 species, but we only eat a handful of them. The problem is that the most popular varieties tend to be overfished and we really do need to look after our oceans.

A few things you can do to help make sure that there will always be plenty more fish in the sea...

Try to eat different fish – don't always choose cod, salmon, or tuna.

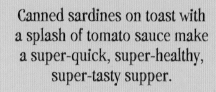

Try to eat oily fish once a week, especially mackerel, herring, and sardines. There are plenty of them in the sea and they contain omega–3 fatty acids, which are good for your heart, brain, skin, and hair.

Canned sardines on toast with a splash of tomato sauce make a super-quick, super-healthy, super-tasty supper.

sardines + whole-wheat toast + blob of tomato sauce + under the broiler for 5 minutes and you're done.

Look out for labels such as the MSC (Marine Stewardship Council). They check that fishermen are using good fishing methods that don't damage the ocean surroundings, the fish stocks, or other species such as birds or dolphins.

Buying Fish

It should smell of the sea, not of rank old fish.

Fresh fish should look firm, shiny, and have bright eyes.

Fish goes bad quickly, so always keep it very cool and cook it on the day you buy it.

Other Seafood

We don't just eat fish, there are…

MOLLUSKS
such as mussels, scallops, and clams, as well as extraordinary creatures like octopus and squid.

CRUSTACEANS
Crab, lobster, prawns, and shrimp taste scrumptiously sweet. They are often gray or blue until we cook them, then they miraculously turn to stunning shades of pink and red.

AND DON'T FORGET THE SEAWEED
In China, Japan, and Korea they've been eating piles of it for centuries. You may have tried some wrapped around a piece of sushi?

We used to eat more seaweed in the West, too, but it's not so common nowadays. Just you wait, seaweed has become big news recently, not just with Asian food but used as a tasty and very healthy seasoning.

You could track some down and sprinkle it on salads and stir-fries for an extra layer of savory flavor.

Cast your net a bit wider and try something new – you may just discover a new favorite.

I'm on the seafood diet…

I see food and I eat it! *

* Well, if you can think of a better fishy joke…

just let minnow!

89

Fish "en Papillote"

(pronounced "on papiyoht")

Here's a great way to prepare fish, sealing in all the fabulous juices and goodness. "En papillote" is French for "in parchment" and sounds a bit more exciting than "fish in a paper bag."

It's fun breaking into the packets at the table, and once you've cracked the simple recipe method you can play around with lots of different variations.

You can always make a quick packet using foil and just pinch the edges together. It doesn't look quite as professional but will still taste great.

---

4 x 16-in (40-cm) squares of waxed paper or parchment paper

olive oil, for brushing

4 medium ripe tomatoes

3½ oz (100 g) green beans, trimmed

salt

4 x 6 oz (160 g) skinned haddock, cod, pollack, hake, or salmon fillets

2 green onions, trimmed and finely sliced

a large handful of parsley or basil leaves, or dill fronds

juice of 1 lemon

---

1 Preheat the oven to 400°F (200°C).

2 Fold each paper square in half and then open it up again so that you have a crease up the middle, like a book. Brush the center of the paper with a little olive oil.

3 Now, cut each tomato into about 5 slices and divide the slices among the papers, placing them just to the right of the crease. Pile on the green beans and season with a pinch of salt.

4 Check your fish for any bones and lay the fillets on top of the vegetables.

5 Sprinkle the green onion slices and herbs over the fish and splash over the lemon juice.

6 Fold the paper over the fish, and, starting at the top, begin folding in about ½ in (1 cm) of the paper just a couple of fingers' width at a time. Keep going in the same direction. Each fold will hold the last one in place — it's a bit like origami. When you get to the bottom of the packet you can twist the paper over in a little tail to fix it.

7 When you are almost ready to eat, put your packets on a baking sheet and cook in the hot oven for 15 minutes. They will puff up with steam.

8 Remove from the oven and slide the packets carefully onto a serving dish or plates and serve at once. It's fun to slash open the packets at the table for a bit of drama — you can use scissors or cut carefully with a knife.

VARY THE VEG Try using carrots, zucchini, snow peas, or peas instead of beans. Use small vegetables, or prepare in slices or matchsticks that will cook through in a short time.

SWAP THE FISH You can use skinned fillets of flat fish, such as plaice or sole, in the recipe but be sure to place them on top of each other so that they don't overcook. Try sandwiching them together with a teaspoon of pesto or tapenade.

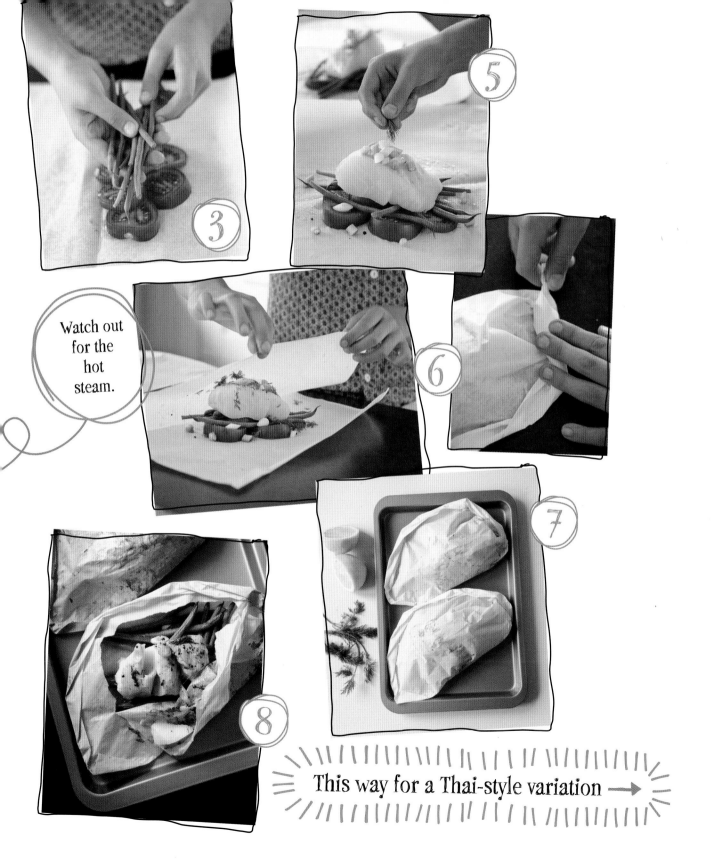

Watch out for the hot steam.

This way for a Thai-style variation →

Thai Scented Fish "en Papillote"

SERVES 4

Now that you've got the fish packet technique under your belt, how about making a spicy Asian version?

4 x 16-in (40-cm) squares
  of waxed paper
  or parchment paper

olive oil, for brushing

5½ oz (150 g) bok choy, cut
  into bite-size pieces

5½ oz (150 g) green beans or
  snow peas, trimmed

salt

4 x 6 oz (160 g) skinned
  haddock, cod, pollack,
  hake, or salmon fillets

2 green onions, trimmed and
  sliced

½-in (1-cm) piece of fresh
  ginger, peeled and chopped

1 garlic clove, peeled and
  finely chopped

2 lemongrass stalks, just
  the tender middle bit,
  finely chopped

1–2 red chiles, chopped ✳

a few leaves of basil or cilantro

juice of 1 lime

2 tbsp soy sauce
  or fish sauce

1 Preheat the oven to 400°F
  (200°C).

2 Make the paper parcels just as
  before (see p. 90).

3 Lay the leaves of bok choy and
  green beans on the paper to the
  right of the crease. Season with
  a pinch of salt and pop the fish
  on top.

4 Sprinkle with all the green onions,
  ginger, garlic, lemongrass, chile,
  and herbs. Squeeze over the lime
  juice and add a splash of soy
  sauce to each. Close the packets
  as before (see p. 90).

5 Bake in the hot oven for
  15 minutes and serve.

It's
a winner
with rice or
noodles.

✳
Check out
how hot
they are!

Broiled Salmon with Honey, Soy, and Orange Marinade

SERVES 4

This marinade is really easy to make but you'll need a bit of help when it comes to the very hot broiler.

The cooked salmon should look charred, almost like it's been on the barbecue. Try it hot or cold, with noodles, rice, steamed vegetables, or even a salad.

You will need some good oven mitts.

1½ lb (700 g) salmon fillet, in one piece

FOR THE MARINADE

3 tbsp runny honey

juice and grated zest of 1 orange

2 tsp grated fresh ginger

4 tbsp soy sauce

---

1 Put all the marinade ingredients together in a jar, close the lid, and give it a good shake.

2 Take a large piece of foil (about 20 x 12 inch/50 x 30 cm) and fold it in half so that you have a double thickness. Fold up about 1 inch (3 cm) around the edges and squeeze at the corners until you have a flat tray just a little bit larger than your fish. Put the tray on a baking dish or pan that fits under your broiler.

3 Now, pour the marinade mixture into the dish and add the salmon, skin side up, so that the flesh is sitting in the liquid. Cover the dish with plastic wrap and leave to marinate for about 30 minutes at room temperature.

4 Heat up your broiler on its hottest setting.

5 Turn the fish over so it is flesh side up, then place the dish under the grill on the highest shelf. Broil for about 6–8 minutes, until the top of the salmon begins to caramelize (color and turn brown).

6 Check the salmon by taking a spoon and pressing it on the thickest part in the middle of the fillet. Once ready, the fish should flake apart and look opaque (not transparent) but still be very juicy. If you have a thick piece of fish it may take a few minutes longer.

7 Serve the fish by spooning it in chunks; it will flake naturally and the skin should stay behind in the foil dish.

8 Tip any juices from the foil tray over the fish before serving with steamed veggies or noodles.

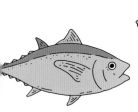

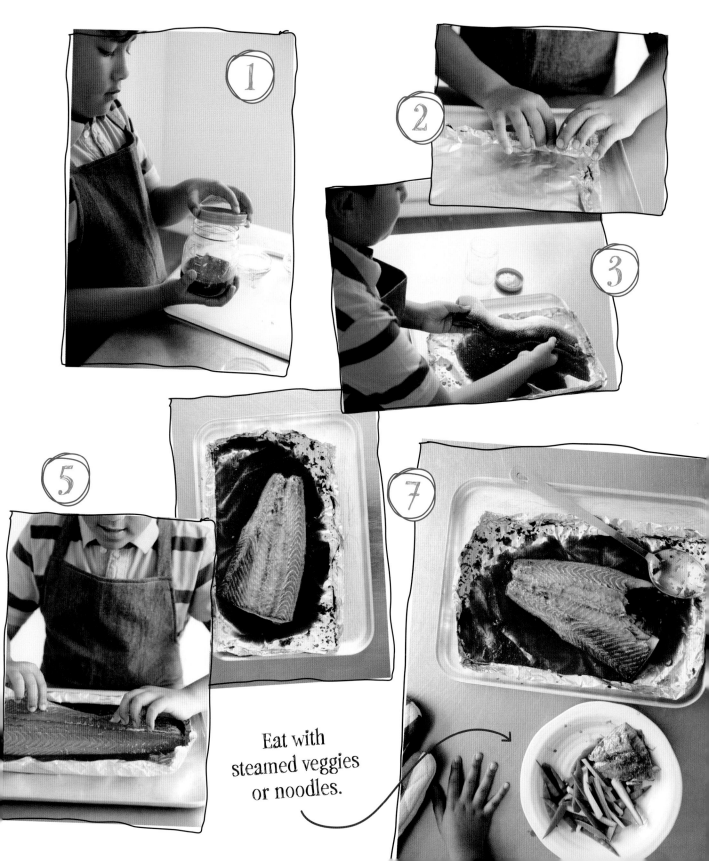

Eat with
steamed veggies
or noodles.

Snacktastic Sticky Chicken Wings

SERVES 4

If you've got time, marinate the wings overnight — they'll taste even better.

The honey, soy, and orange marinade used for the broiled salmon (see p. 94) is amazing with chicken too. Just leave out the orange juice, but keep the zest, so that you have a really sticky mixture.

12–16 chicken wings

1 x Honey, Soy, and Orange Marinade (minus the orange juice) – see p. 94

salt and pepper

1. Ask the butcher or a helpful adult to cut off the chicken wing tips for you.

2. Make up the marinade in a small pitcher. Put the chicken wings into a shallow dish or a resealable freezer bag and pour over the marinade. Turn the wings over to get them all sticky, then wash your hands. Cover with plastic wrap (or seal the bag) and chill in the fridge for at least 3 hours or, better still, overnight.

3. Preheat the oven to 400°F (200°C).

4. Spread the wings out on a non-stick roasting pan and cook in the oven for 20 minutes. Turn the wings over with tongs and cook for another 20 minutes until browned and crispy.

5. Remove from the oven (use oven mitts). Season with a little salt and pepper and dive in. They're great with a leafy salad, quinoa salad (see p. 50), noodles, or stir-fried vegetables with rice.

Spice It Up

with a pinch of cayenne pepper.

Try

using chicken drumsticks. Make sure that the chicken is well cooked before serving.

Or just munch with your fingers right away.

Is the chicken cooked?

Chicken can give you food poisoning if it is not properly cooked. Once the pink, shiny flesh has turned white and firm, it is ready to eat.

Meat is a Treat

We don't need meat to survive, but it is a very good source of protein. Remember that proteins are like the body's building blocks — we need them to grow and repair our cells. Not everyone eats meat; there are plenty of vegetarians in the world who get their protein from eggs, dairy, beans, and nuts, but lots of us do love to eat meat.

More than 50% of the world's pork is munched in China; well, there are 1½ billion people to feed!

Many different animals are eaten around the world, and these four lead the way.

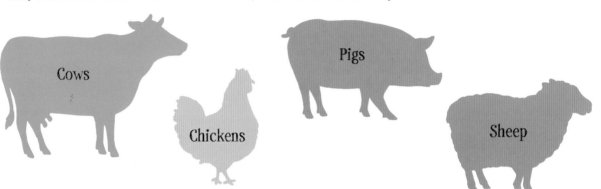

Cows

Chickens

Pigs

Sheep

More pork is eaten than any other meat. It's not just about pork chops; don't forget that ham, bacon, and most sausages are all made from pork.

Eating some meat regularly is good for us as long as we eat plenty of vegetables too, but unhealthy processed meats such as sausages, ham, bacon, and salami (which are packed with salt) should be occasional treats.

Meat – the future

The world population is growing and so is our appetite for meat. We have to grow crops to feed all these animals; it's going to be impossible for us to keep up with the demand while looking after our planet and caring properly for the animals.

How can we help? Some thoughts to chew over with your friends.

⭐ Fancy a bug burger? More than 2 billion people in the world eat insects as part of their daily diet. Farming bugs is better for the planet than farming mammals.

Would you eat grasshoppers or worms?

⭐ Scientists are experimenting with growing meat in laboratories — it's called in vitro meat or shmeat. It will use less energy to produce this meat, and we don't need to worry about animal cruelty, but it's not natural.

Will you be first in line for a shmeaty shepherd's pie?

⭐ How about only eating meat once or twice a week? You will be able to afford good-quality meat from animals that are well cared for.

Will the world follow your lead?

⭐ What about becoming a vegetarian?

Would you miss your meat too much?

Making the most of your meat...

Good-quality meat from animals that have been carefully farmed is expensive. It makes sense to really enjoy the good stuff in smaller quantities when we can, and eat plant-based meals the rest of the time.

Respecting the animals that we rear and eat is important, so the last thing we want to do is waste anything. A roast is a great way to enjoy a family meal and give you plenty of leftovers as well as some bones for stock; a chicken is a very good place to start.

How to roast a chicken

1 Preheat the oven to 375°F (190°C).

2 Check how much your chicken weighs and put it straight into a roasting pan.

3 Look inside the chicken for any giblets. They often come in a plastic bag — melted plastic won't taste very good! If you have some then put them aside for making stock.

These are other edible bits from the bird such as the neck, heart, and liver.

4 Cut a lemon in half and rub the skin with the lemon flesh, then pop the halves inside the bird. You could put a few sprigs of fresh rosemary or thyme in too.

5 Pour 2 tablespoons olive oil over the chicken and then roll the bird over in the roasting pan to cover it in oil. Place the chicken breast side up and sprinkle over 1 teaspoon salt.

6 Roast in the oven for 20 minutes per 1 lb (45 minutes per 1 kg).

7 Make sure that the chicken is completely cooked through — poke a skewer into the thigh and check that the juice is clear and not bloody. Chicken flesh should be opaque, with no sign of blood, when it is ready.

8 Now that you have your scrumptious roast chicken out of the oven, leave it for 10 minutes to rest before getting an adult to carve it up for serving.

Not shiny and see-through-ish.

CHALLENGE

Make your roast chicken last for 3 meals

Don't eat too much... a few bits of leftover cold chicken will be delicious in any of the leafy or grain salads in this book or popped into a sandwich. That leaves the bones to make a stock; you could finish up with the Chicken Noodle Broth (p. 64).

Try the 3-meal challenge at home with other pieces of meat too

One-pot Chicken

SERVES 4

→ Who does?

If you don't like doing the dishes, then this is your recipe. Everything goes into one big dish in the oven. It's so simple and there are loads of different variations. You'll just need some good bread to soak up the juices.

3 tbsp olive oil, canola oil, or other vegetable oil

1 tbsp butter

2 medium onions

4–8 chicken thighs, depending on size, on the bone and with skin

½ tsp salt and plenty of pepper

+ one of the choices on p. 103

Chicken thighs are so much juicier than breasts in this dish.

1 Preheat the oven to 350°F (180°C).

2 Take a large ovenproof dish (mine measures 10 x 12 inch/ 25 x 30 cm) and spoon in the oil and butter.

3 Cut the onions in half leaving the root on, then peel and then slice them (see p. 13). Put the onions into the dish.

4 Trim any flappy bits of skin from the chicken thighs. Add the thighs to the dish, then turn everything gently with your fingers in the oil. Leave the thighs skin side up.

5 Sprinkle the chicken with the salt and a good grind of pepper and put the dish in the oven for 10 minutes.

6 Now take your chicken wherever you want in the world (see pages 102–103). Just add the rest of the ingredients and pop the dish back in the oven for 30 more minutes, or until the chicken is cooked through. Make sure that the chicken is always skin side up so the skin gets crispy.

7 Check that the chicken is cooked. Then taste the juices; you might need a bit more salt and pepper.

Go and wash your hands, the knife, and the chopping board now.

Always check that the chicken is properly cooked through. Turn over a thigh and cut in next to the bone; there should be no sign of blood or raw-looking flesh.

Recipe continues on p. 102 →

6

Spanish Chicken

One-pot Chicken recipe +

2 red or yellow bell peppers, seeded and sliced

3 medium tomatoes, cut into quarters

12 pitted green or black olives (optional)

1 heaping teaspoon Spanish sweet smoked paprika

2 x 14-oz (400-g) can lima beans, drained

1. Just add everything to the chicken dish. Take care: it will be hot. Give it a stir and then lift the chicken pieces with a spoon or tongs to sit skin side up on the top.

2. Place back in the oven for 30–40 minutes, or until the chicken is cooked through.

Southern French Chicken

One-pot Chicken recipe +

1 tablespoon Dijon mustard

2 tablespoons wine vinegar

²/₃ cup (150 ml) crème fraîche

3 medium tomatoes, cut into quarters

2 x 14-oz (400-g) can flageolet beans, drained

leaves from 3 large sprigs of tarragon

Save a few leaves to sprinkle on the top of the finished dish.

1. Stir together the mustard, vinegar and crème fraîche, then add this with the rest of the ingredients to the chicken dish. Make sure that the chicken is sitting on the top.

2. Place back in the oven for 30–40 minutes, or until the chicken is cooked through. Sprinkle with more tarragon before serving.

Indian Chicken
call it a curry if you like

One-pot Chicken recipe +

2 x 14-oz (400-g) can chickpeas, drained

1 small or ½ large cauliflower, broken into florets

2–3 tablespoons curry powder

half of a 14-oz (400-g) can coconut milk

a large handful of cilantro leaves

a lime, cut into 4 wedges

Use the other half of the can in a smoothie.

1. Add the chickpeas and cauliflower to the hot chicken dish and sprinkle over the spices. Using a spoon, turn the vegetables over in the spices, then put the chicken pieces on top and pour in the coconut milk.

2. Place back in the oven for 30–40 minutes, or until the chicken is cooked through. Sprinkle with cilantro and give everyone a slice of lime to squeeze over.

Great with flatbread to soak up the juices.

MEATBALLS

Don't forget to wash your hands before and after handling raw meat.

Rolling ground meat into balls with your favorite spices, herbs, and seasonings is soooo simple. Once you've got the hang of the technique, you can experiment with recipes from all around the world.

Simple Meatballs

MAKES ABOUT 20/ SERVES 4

Wet hands stop the meatball mixture sticking as you roll.

1 thick slice of white bread, crusts removed

1/2 cup (100 ml) milk

8 oz (225 g) ground beef

8 oz (225 g) ground pork

1 onion, grated

3 tbsp finely chopped flat-leaf parsley

a large pinch of salt

a grind of pepper

2 tbsp olive oil

You may want your swimming goggles? You might cry.

1 Rip the bread into a few pieces and put them into a small bowl with the milk. Leave to soak.

2 Next, mix up the meat, onion, parsley, and a bit of seasoning in a large bowl.

3 Mash up the bread and milk mixture with a fork and pour this into the meat mixture.

4 Now, mix all the ingredients really well using your very clean hands.

5 You need to check out the taste before you go rolling all those balls. So take a tablespoon of the mixture and squash it in the palm of your hands into a flat cake — like a mini burger.

6 Heat up a large frying pan with the olive oil and fry the tester for a few minutes on each side until cooked through. Allow to cool for a couple of minutes and then taste... What do you think? Does it need more salt or pepper? Add some if you think so.

7 Roll the rest of the mixture into balls about the size of a walnut and put them on a tray. Try to keep them all the same size; then they will take the same time to cook.

8 Heat up the pan again over high heat and carefully add about half of the meatballs. Allow them to brown a little, then very carefully roll them over to color the underside too. Spoon them out onto a plate and brown the rest of the raw balls.

9 Now, add them all back to the pan, turn down the heat and cook gently for about 5 more minutes until firm. TEST a ball by cutting it in half. If the meat is still pink, cook for a couple of minutes longer.

② ③ ④ ⑦ ⑧

Steam must be able
to escape otherwise
the meat will sweat
instead of brown.

Other meatball styles → → →

Italian Meatballs
Makes about 20/ serves 4

1 x SIMPLE MEATBALL RECIPE + add a pinch of DRIED OREGANO to the meat mixture along with the PARSLEY before you begin rolling the balls.

Serve the meatballs with tomato sauce (see p. 83) and a bowl of cooked spaghetti or short pasta such as penne or fusilli.

Grate plenty of Parmesan or pecorino cheese over the top.

Cheddar's fine too.

Spanish Meatballs
Makes about 20/ serves 4

1 x SIMPLE MEATBALL RECIPE + add 1 teaspoon SWEET SMOKED PAPRIKA and a good pinch of ground CINNAMON to the meat mixture along with the salt and pepper.

Once the meatballs are cooked you can add the tomato sauce (see p. 83) to the pan and heat everything up together.

Serve with crusty bread.

Moroccan Meatballs
Makes about 20/ serves 4

1 x SIMPLE MEATBALL RECIPE using ground lamb instead of the pork and beef + add 2 heaped teaspoons RAS-AL-HANOUT to the meat mixture before you begin making the balls.

Serve with couscous, or Moroccan tomato sauce and chickpeas; see p. 85.

NO RAS-AL-HANOUT?
Well, 1 teaspoon ground cumin, ½ teaspoon ground ginger and ½ teaspoon ground cinnamon will be just fine.

Vietnamese Pork Meatballs

MAKES ABOUT 20

These spicy Southeast Asian meatballs are made in a similar way to all the other meatballs in the book except that you will leave out the bread and milk and use a couple of egg whites to hold the mixture together instead.

1 lb (450 g) ground pork

3 green onions, trimmed and finely chopped

1 garlic clove, peeled and crushed

¾-in (2-cm) piece of fresh ginger, peeled and grated

2 egg whites

1–2 tsp cold water

a large pinch of salt

a grind of pepper

2 tbsp vegetable oil

1. Put the pork, green onions, garlic, and ginger into a large mixing bowl.

2. Mix the egg whites and cold water together in a small bowl with a fork, then pour it in with the meat mixture.

3. Add the salt and pepper and mix everything together really well.

4. Now for the test run. Shape up a tiny disk of mixture (like a mini-burger) and fry it in a large pan with the vegetable oil. Allow to cool a little before tasting. Does the meatball need any more salt or pepper?

5. Now you're ready to roll. You want to make about 20 walnut-size balls.

6. Place the meatballs on a baking sheet, cover, and chill the meatballs, if you have time, and then fry them in 2 batches so they brown nicely and put them all back in the pan to cook through.

7. Serve the meatballs with rice and maybe some steamed vegetables, or try the suggestion here...

Don't forget: Wet hands stop the mixture from sticking.

Hot and Spicy Dipping Sauce

1 garlic clove, peeled and crushed

4 tbsp fish sauce (or soy sauce will do)

juice of 1 lime

3 tbsp superfine sugar

1–2 hot chiles, sliced or diced very finely (!!!! Danger HOT – add a little at a time and taste!)

Stir all the sauce ingredients together in a bowl, adding a tiny bit of chile at a time.

The sauce should be sweet, sour, salty, and hot.

D.I.Y. Vietnamese Nems – pork and salad rolls

20 lettuce leaves, such as iceberg or Little Gem

40 mint leaves

Set out the pork meatballs, salad leaves, mint, and dipping sauce in the middle of the table.

Let everyone dive in. Roll up and eat with your fingers.

By now
you must be
a meatball
pro!

ITALIAN → FRENCH ←

Ragù, Ragout
or Ground Meat Stew

A really tasty ground meat stew can be the centerpiece of so many dishes. Learn to make this one recipe and you'll have loads of great supper options.

2 tbsp olive oil or butter

4 slices of unsmoked bacon, cut into small pieces

1 onion, peeled and finely chopped

1 carrot, peeled and finely chopped

1 celery stalk, finely chopped

2 garlic cloves, peeled and crushed

1 lb 2oz (500 g) ground beef

1 cup (200 ml) whole milk

1 x 14-oz (400-g) can diced tomatoes

2 tbsp tomato paste

½ cup (100 ml) red wine (or beef stock)

salt and pepper

1 bay leaf

1 Heat the olive oil in a pan over medium heat, add the bacon, and fry for about 2 minutes.

2 Add the onion, carrot, and celery to the pan and cook, stirring once in a while, for about 10 minutes, or until the onion looks soft and almost see-through or "translucent."

3 Stir in the garlic and, once you can really smell it, add the ground meat. Crumble the meat in with your fingers so that it doesn't stay in big lumps. Wash your hands well afterwards. Cook over high heat for about 5 minutes.

There's a handy word.

4 Next, pour in the milk and cook slowly for 10 minutes before adding the tomatoes, tomato paste, and wine. Add a pinch of salt, a grind of black pepper, and the bay leaf. Allow the mixture to heat up and bubble, then cover the pan with a lid and turn the heat down to a very low simmer for at least 45 minutes.

5 Don't forget to taste before serving. Remember to add seasoning slowly and carefully.

If the mixture gets a bit too dry and begins to stick to the bottom of the pan, just add a half of a small glass of water and give it a good stir.

In an Italian kitchen the ragù often simmers on the stove for an entire day and the flavor just gets better and better. Try putting the covered pan (ovenproof of course!) into an oven preheated to 250°F (130°C) for 3 or 4 hours.

And once you've cracked the recipe, how about ...

Extra bits in your ragù?

Add some chopped-up butternut squash at the same time as the meat. It will soften and make the sauce feel creamy.

⬇

Add some diced zucchini along with a handful of chopped parsley or basil about 2 minutes before you finish cooking the ragù.

⬇

Stir in a 14-oz (400-g) can drained cannellini beans and a pinch of finely chopped rosemary.

Things to do with your ragù

Serve as Bolognese sauce with cooked spaghetti or short pasta, such as penne or fusilli, and plenty of grated Parmesan cheese.

⬇

Eat alongside a baked potato.

⬇

Or transform it into...

Chili con Carne
or
Cottage Pie

Here's how ↘

Chili con Carne

Once you've made the ragù a few times you may feel like spicing it up. Remember to go very carefully with the chili powder. You can always serve some extra hot sauce at the table for the would-be flamethrowers.

Ragù + Beans + Spices + Cilantro = Chili con Carne

keep the leaves to garnish later

- 1 x Ragù recipe (see p. 110)
- 1 tsp ground cumin
- 1 tsp oregano
- ¼ tsp chili powder (you can always add a little more next time around)
- a small bunch of cilantro
- 1 x 14-oz (400-g) can red kidney beans or black beans, drained

1 Make your ragù (see p. 110). Fry the bacon and vegetables, then add the ground cumin, oregano, and chili powder at the same time as the garlic. Once you can really smell the spices (and the chili powder might make you gasp a little), add the ground meat.

2 Cook your meat for a few minutes just like you did before.

3 Now chop up the cilantro stalks really finely and add those to the pan along with the canned tomatoes, the tomato paste, the wine (or beef stock), and salt and pepper.

4 Simmer for 30 minutes then add the beans. Cook for another 15 minutes and then serve with any combination of the following:

Can you take the heat?

If your food is too hot and spicy, take a large spoonful of yogurt or a swig of milk. Water just washes the burning capsaicin around the mouth whereas the casein protein in dairy products binds with the capsaicin oil and washes away.

Sour cream / Guacamole / grated Cheddar cheese

+

Baked potato / rice / tortilla

+

Slice of lime

How about a refreshing Lassi drink to cool those taste buds (see p. 35)?

Mashed Potatoes

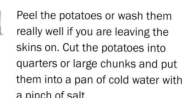

SERVES 4

Try leaving the peel on your potatoes for extra flavor and goodness.

Use oven mitts – don't forget that steam can burn.

2 lb (900 g) large potatoes

a good pinch of salt

4 tbsp butter

²⁄₃ cup (150 ml) milk

pepper (optional)

1 Peel the potatoes or wash them really well if you are leaving the skins on. Cut the potatoes into quarters or large chunks and put them into a pan of cold water with a pinch of salt.

2 Put the pan over high heat and bring the water to a boil. Turn the heat to medium and boil the potatoes for about 15 minutes.

3 Poke a piece of potato with a knife or skewer — the center should feel soft. Otherwise carry on cooking for a minute or two longer and check again.

4 Pour the potatoes into a colander in the sink to drain.

5 Give the colander a shake to help dry off the potatoes and then pour them back into the hot pan. Add the butter and allow the heat of the pan to begin melting it. Now mash the potatoes until they're lump free.

6 Pour in the milk and stir the mash with a wooden spoon until it's creamy and smooth.

7 Taste and add more salt and little bit of pepper, if you like.

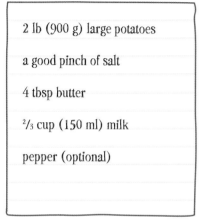

Try stirring in some sour cream, cream cheese, grated cheese, or a handful of chopped chives.

Cottage Pie

SERVES 4

Ragù +
Mashed Potato =
Cottage Pie

1 x Ragù recipe (see p. 110)

2 tbsp Worcestershire sauce

1 x Mashed Potatoes recipe
(see opposite)

2 tbsp dried bread crumbs

2 tbsp butter

1. Preheat the oven to 375°F (190°C).

2. Cook the simple ragù recipe on p. 110 and add 2 tablespoons Worcestershire sauce. Remove the bay leaf.

3. Take an ovenproof dish (about 10 in/25 cm square). Now spoon the meat mixture into the dish; it should come about halfway up the sides.

4. Spoon over the mashed potatoes. Go carefully, if you drop them all at once, the potatoes will sink into the meat mixture. Spread out the potatoes with the back of a fork, leaving the surface quite rough.

5. Sprinkle with bread crumbs and then chop up the butter into tiny pieces and sprinkle over the top.

6. Place in the oven for 30 minutes to heat through and crisp up and brown the top. (If you made the dish earlier and it's coming from the fridge, this will take 40 minutes.)

Champ

SERVES 4

Don't let the milk boil. It froths up and makes a hideous mess.

A good old Irish dish.

1 x Mashed Potatoes recipe
(see opposite)

5 green onions, trimmed and
sliced

salt and pepper

1. Cook your potatoes as you did before, and while you are mashing them with the butter just heat up the milk with the sliced green onions in a small pan.

2. Beat the milk and green onions into the mash and taste. Add salt and pepper, if you like.

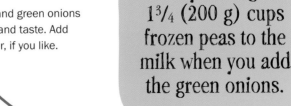

Try adding
1³/₄ (200 g) cups
frozen peas to the
milk when you add
the green onions.

Baked Potatoes

SERVES 4

Baked potatoes aren't just tasty and filling, they're good for you too. Make sure you eat the skin as it's packed with precious fiber.

That's the bit that stops you getting hungry again too quickly.

1 medium potato per person

1 tsp olive oil

½ tsp salt

butter or extra-virgin olive oil, to serve

1. Preheat the oven to 400°F (200°C).

2. Wash and dry the potatoes, then cut through the skin down one side, where you will open up the potato later.

3. Put a teaspoon of olive oil into the palm of your hand and rub the skins all over. Now sprinkle a pinch of salt over the potatoes; the oil will help it to stick.

4. Place on a baking sheet in the hot oven and bake for 1–1½ hours depending on the size of the potatoes.

5. Test a potato with a fork. When it is ready it should be crisp on the outside and soft within.

6. Split open each potato and serve with a bit of butter or a dash of extra-virgin olive oil. Or...

This is the trick for crispy skins.

Twice-baked Potatoes

SERVES 4

These are a meal in themselves, especially when served with green salad or slaw.

It's your choice.

1. Once your potatoes are baked, as above, let them cool for at least 10 minutes. Keep the oven on.

2. Now cut them in half and scoop out about two-thirds of the flesh with a spoon. Be careful: the potatoes will still be hot and you don't want to rip the skin.

3. Mash up the potato flesh with your filling.

(PER POTATO)

1 oz (25 g) cheese (cream cheese, Cheddar, goat's cheese, or blue cheese)

a few chopped chives or a sliced green onion

1 tbsp butter

4. Spoon the cheesy mixture back into the potatoes, sprinkle with a pinch of extra cheese, and pop them back into the oven for about 15 minutes, or until heated through.

You could add other bits, such as chopped ham or cooked bacon or a spoonful of pesto. Have fun. Experiment!

with Slaw (p. 38),
Guacamole (p. 52),
bean salad (p. 44),
Ragù (p. 110),
Chili con Carne (p. 114),
Designer Baked Beans (p. 85)...
Oh, there are so
many options!

Bountiful Baking

savory bread and teatime treats

Irish Soda Bread

MAKES 1 LARGE LOAF

This is wonderful beginner's bread — it's so quick and easy to make. Soda bread has no yeast: it's the bicarbonate of soda that creates the gas to make it rise.

A bit of kitchen chemistry

Put alkaline baking soda and acidic lemon juice together and you get a chemical reaction which creates lots of gas (carbon dioxide). This gas is what makes your bread rise.

3½ cups (500 g) whole-wheat flour and about 3 tbsp extra for dusting

1 tsp salt

1 heaped tsp baking soda

1 tbsp lemon juice

1¾ cups (400 ml) milk

1 tbsp dark molasses

2 tsp honey

1. Preheat the oven to 400°F (200°C).

2. Put the flour, salt, and baking soda together into a large dry bowl and use your hands to mix them thoroughly. Make a big well in the middle of the flour.

3. Add the lemon juice to your milk, then spoon in the molasses and honey too. Give the milk a good stir with a fork until the molasses and honey have almost dissolved.

4. Pour the milk mixture into the flour bowl and stir with a wooden spoon until all the dry flour has disappeared and you have a really sticky dough.

5. Dust your work surface or clean table with about 3 tablespoons extra flour and, using a spoon, plop out the dough into the middle of it. Cover your hands in flour off the table and pat the dough into a ball shape. Carefully turn the dough over.

6. Sprinkle a baking sheet with about 1 tablespoon of flour and place the ball of dough on top. Now flatten the ball until you have a disk about 2 in (5 cm) thick.

7. Make a deep cross in the bread, cutting about halfway through the dough, and put in the oven straightaway.

8. Bake for 50 minutes, or until the bread sounds hollow when tapped underneath.

9. Leave to cool on a rack.

It'll be very soft.

The old Irish story goes that you cut the cross in the top to bless the bread and let the fairies out!

How about celebrating St Patrick's Day, on March 17, with a loaf?

⑥

SPOTTY DOG

Add a handful of raisins to the dough – just fling them into the bowl with your flour at the beginning of the recipe.

SUPERSEEDS SODA

Add 3 tablespoons of seeds, such as pumpkin, sunflower, sesame, or poppy seeds. You can choose your mixture. Mix them in with the flour at the beginning of the recipe.

LIGHT AS A LEPRECHAUN

Use plain white flour instead of whole-wheat for a much lighter loaf.

THE REAL THING

If you want to be really Irish about your soda bread, then you can use buttermilk instead of the milk and lemon juice.

Soda bread is especially tasty with butter and honey, but why not try loading it up with Hummus (see p. 54), Guacamole (see p. 52), or cream cheese and smoked salmon for a healthy snack or lunch?

⑦

A FEW IDEAS FOR AN OPEN SANDWICH

Scandinavians love these. They can look pretty impressive too.

Torn herbs / seedy sprinkles / chopped nuts
+
Fresh peas / chopped cucumber / diced tomato
+
Creamy cheese / hummus / guacamole
+
Slice of bread or toast

Banana Bread

MAKES 1 LOAF

Here's a great way to use up any overripe bananas. It's not bread at all; it's more of a teatime treat really, but you do bake it in a loaf pan. You don't need an electric whisk or mixer for this recipe, but a balloon whisk is handy.

The easiest way is to cut a piece of paper that fits the length of your pan and then overlap the sides too.

You will need a 9x5-inch (23x13-cm) loaf pan

²/₃ cup (150 ml) light olive oil, sunflower oil, or melted butter, plus a little extra for greasing the loaf pan

½ cup (75 g) hazelnuts or any other nuts, such as walnuts, almonds, or pecans

1 cup (200 g) firmly packed light brown sugar

2 eggs

1 tsp vanilla extract

3 bananas, peeled

1²/₃ cups (225 g) self-rising flour

1 Preheat the oven to 325°F (170°C).

2 Line your loaf pan with parchment paper. Grease the ends of the pan with butter or oil.

3 Roast your hazelnuts (or whatever nuts you are using) on a baking sheet in the oven for about 5 minutes until they smell especially nutty and toasty. Keep an eye on them as nuts burn very easily. Leave them to cool and then chop them really roughly.

4 Pour the oil (or melted butter) into a big bowl with the sugar, eggs, and vanilla extract. Now whisk or mix together with a fork until everything is well combined.

5 Put the bananas into another bowl and mash them with the back of a fork; don't worry about getting them smooth, it's good to leave a few lumps. (You should have about 1½ cups (12 oz/ 350 g) mashed banana.)

6 Add the mashed bananas and nuts to the egg mixture and give it a stir.

7 Pour the flour into the cake mixture and beat together with a wooden spoon or balloon whisk until all the dry, white specks of flour have just disappeared, then pour the cake mixture into the loaf pan RIGHT AWAY and place in the middle of your hot oven.

8 Bake for about 50 minutes until firm. Test with a skewer by pushing the point into the center of the cake. Pull it out. If the skewer is moist but clean, your banana bread is ready; if there's any sign of custardy batter then the cake needs a bit more time.

If you're worried about the top of the cake getting too dark, then pop a piece of foil over the top.

A bit of kitchen chemistry

There's no time to hang around because the baking soda and cream of tartar in the self-rising flour will begin to react and bubble as soon as they meet the wet banana mixture. You need to trap the air bubbles as the cake bakes.

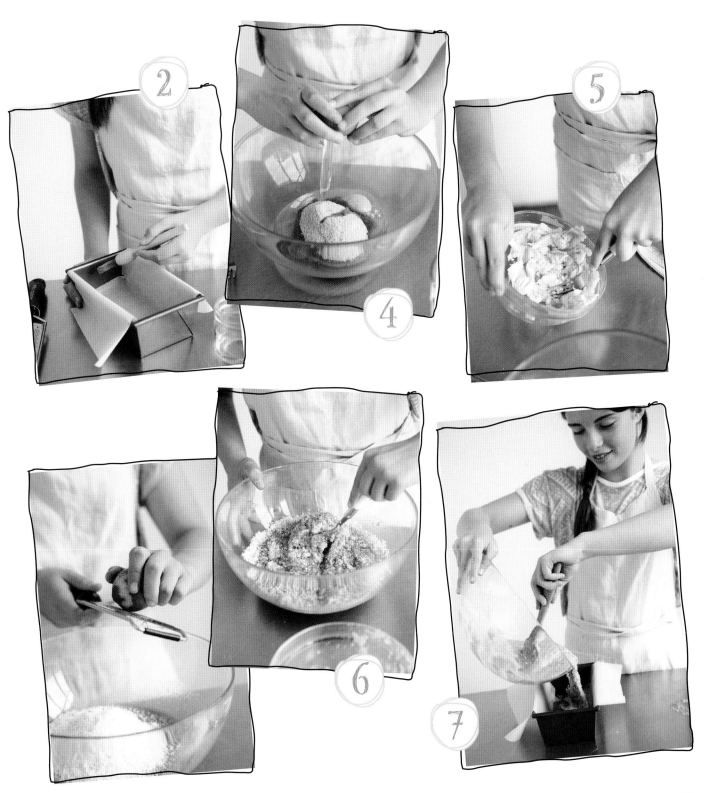

Banana and Chocolate Bread

Banana bread recipe +
chunky chocolate chips =
chocolatey treat

Leave out the nuts and add
3½ oz (100 g) dark
or milk chocolate

Chop or break the chocolate
up into pieces about the size of
your little fingernail.

Stir them into the cake mixture
at the same time as the bananas.

You could pull
all the stops
out and add the
nuts too.

THE WORD
BANANA COMES
FROM THE ARABIC
WORD "BANAN,"
WHICH MEANS
FINGER.

Banana, Coconut, and Lime Drizzle Bread

Banana bread recipe +
coconut and lime =
truly tropical flavor

2 limes

1 cup (100 g) unsweetened
shredded dried coconut
instead of the nuts

½ cup (85 g) superfine sugar

Remove the zest from the
limes using a fine grater.

Stir the coconut and
the lime zest into the
cake mixture at the same
time as the mashed bananas.

Now for the drizzle.

Squeeze the lime juice into a bowl
with the superfine sugar and stir
well with a fork. Once the banana
bread is out of the oven, but still in
the pan, prick the top all over with
a skewer or toothpick and then
pour over the lime drizzle.

Try to leave all
the white pith
behind; it tastes
really bitter.

Gingerbread Cookies

MAKES ABOUT 20

These are crispy cookies rather than the softer, spongier gingerbread you often find. They are delicious any time of the year but do look really Christmassy if you decorate them simply and hang them from a branch.

2¹⁄₂ cups (350 g) all-purpose flour, plus a little extra for dusting

1 tsp baking soda

2 tsp ground ginger

7 tbsp butter

1 cup (175 g) firmly packed light brown sugar

1 medium egg

4 tbsp light corn syrup

1 Preheat the oven to 375°F (190°C).

2 Sift the flour, baking soda, and ginger into a large mixing bowl.

3 Cut the butter into small pieces about the size of your little fingernail and stir them into the flour mixture.

4 Rub the butter pieces into the flour between your fingertips so that they break into tiny crumblike flakes. Keep going until all the oily buttery bits have disappeared; it will take a while. Now stir in the sugar.

5 Break the whole egg into a mug and add the syrup. Give it a good stir with a fork until well mixed then pour this into the bowl with the rest of the ingredients.

6 Begin stirring with a large spoon and then work the mixture with your hands, gathering it together and squeezing it until it sticks together like a dough. Divide the dough in half.

7 Dust your work surface or clean table with a spoonful of flour. Dust the rolling pin too and get rolling.

8 Once the cookie dough is about ¼ in (5 mm) thick you can begin cutting. Use one cookie cutter shape, or several different shapes; it's up to you!

9 Line two baking sheets with parchment paper and arrange the cookies, leaving a thin gap around them. Bake in the hot oven for about 10 minutes until slightly darker and dry looking.

10 Remove from the oven. Leave for 2 minutes to firm up on the baking sheets, then lift the cookies carefully with a spatula onto a wire rack to cool.

11 Decorate as you wish! Keep in an airtight container for a couple of weeks.

Traditional Gingerbread People

There's nothing new about gingerbread people – we have been eating them since Medieval times, more than 500 years ago.

Cut out your cookies using a gingerbread person cookie cutter and place them on a baking sheet lined with parchment paper.

Push 2 currants into the dough for eyes, and 3 more for buttons. Mark a smile in the dough with a skewer and bake in the hot oven for 10 minutes.

Double Gingers

Roughly chop enough crystallized ginger to make $^1/_4$ cup. Add the ginger to the batter with the egg and syrup mixture in step 5 of the Gingerbread People recipe on page 130.

Christmas Cookies

 A fab present for teachers.

The original gingerbread recipe works well for festive cookies, but if you want to make more traditional Christmas cookies you could try this little twist.

Add $^1/_2$ teaspoon ground cinnamon and a good pinch of ground nutmeg and ground cloves at the beginning of the recipe along with the ginger. Use cookie-cutter shapes such as snowflakes, hearts, and stars to make your cookies. As soon as they are out of the oven, and still hot, use a skewer to make a hole for hanging the cookies.

Decorate with icing (see p. 143) and edible dragées. Use simple ribbon or striped baker's twine to hang the cookies.

Remember that lots of colors look fun, but pure white and silver can have a big impact too.

Chocolate and Beet Muffins

MAKES 12

It may seem a bit bonkers to include grated vegetables in a muffin recipe, but they make the texture fabulously juicy. You've probably tasted carrot cake before, which doesn't seem like eating vegetables at all, so give these a try.

1 cup (200 g) firmly packed light brown sugar

7 tbsp vegetable oil (or light olive oil or melted butter), plus a little extra for greasing the muffin pan if needed

2 medium eggs

4 tbsp plain yogurt

scant 1½ cups (200 g) self-rising flour

3 tbsp cocoa powder

7 oz beets (200 g), washed really well

3½ oz (100 g) semisweet chocolate

Choc chips are great.

1 Preheat the oven to 325°F (170°C).

2 Grease a 12-hole muffin pan or line the wells with paper liners, if you prefer.

3 Take a large bowl and mix together the sugar, oil or butter, eggs, and yogurt with a wooden spoon until smooth.

4 Put the flour and cocoa powder into a separate bowl.

5 Cut the stalk off the beet and grate it, skin and all, using the rough, largest holes on your grater.

6 Chop up the chocolate into raisin-size pieces (if you are not using chips).

7 Pour the flour, chocolate, and beet into the bowl with the egg mixture and give it a stir. Don't worry about a few lumps; as soon as the white flecks of flour have disappeared you can spoon the mixture into the muffin pan or paper liners.

8 Bake in the hot oven for 25–30 minutes until the muffins are well risen. Test with a skewer or toothpick to see that the middle is fully baked (poke the skewer in, and when you pull it out check for uncooked gloopy mixture — if the skewer or toothpick is clean your muffins are ready).

9 Cool a little on a wire rack (but muffins are delicious eaten warm).

Watch your fingers and wear an apron — beets stain.

Too much mixing = heavy, chewy muffins.

There's an old saying that if a man and a woman eat from the same beet they will fall in love. Better watch out who you share your muffins with!

Cheesy Zucchini and Corn Muffins

MAKES 12

These use the same method as sweet muffins: keep the wet and dry ingredients apart until everything is ready to go, stir briefly, and bake. That's all there is to it.

The self-rising flour will begin to puff up as soon as it hits the moisture – you want that rising to happen in the oven, not the mixing bowl.

7 tbsp olive, canola, or sunflower oil, plus a little extra for greasing the tray if needed

2 medium eggs

4 tbsp plain yogurt

scant 1½ cups (200 g) self-rising flour

7 oz zucchini (200 g), washed really well

3½ oz (100 g) mature Cheddar cheese, or a mix of Cheddar and Parmesan cheese

¾ cup (100 g) corn, frozen or canned

2 tbsp pumpkin or sunflower seeds

1 Preheat the oven to 325°F (170°C).

2 Grease a 12-hole muffin pan or line the wells with paper liners, if you prefer.

3 Put the oil, eggs, and yogurt into a large bowl and mix well with a fork.

4 Keep the flour in a separate bowl.

5 Grate the zucchini and cheese on the coarse side of your grater.

← No grated fingers, thank you!!

6 Tip the flour, zucchini, cheese, and corn into the bowl with the egg mixture and give it a quick stir. Spoon the mixture into the muffin wells or liners straightaway and sprinkle with the seeds.

7 Bake in the hot oven for 25–30 minutes, or until the muffins are ready.

Give them the skewer test.

Other ways for other days

Swap cheeses. Any hard cheese will work.

Try using grated pumpkin, carrot, or beet instead of the zucchini.

Add nuts instead of the corn.

A teaspoon of finely chopped thyme or rosemary would be good here too.

Sprinkle with rolled oats instead of the seeds.

For super-healthy muffins, use self-rising whole-wheat flour instead of white.

THE CAKE Recipe

You can make loads of different cakes with just one recipe and one set of cake pans. Master this method and you'll know that you'll have a fab result every time.

You really need an electric mixer for this, either a handheld or a stand mixer, or your arm might just drop off with all the mixing.

butter wrappers or 1 tbsp vegetable oil for greasing

scant 1 cup (200 g) softened butter

1 cup (200 g) superfine sugar

4 medium eggs (at room temperature)

scant 1½ cups (200 g) self-rising flour

1 tsp baking powder

2 tbsp milk

+ filling + topping (see p. 142–143) OR just 5 tbsp of any tasty jam

1. Position a rack in the middle of the oven and preheat the oven to 350°F (180°C).

2. Grease and line the base of two 8-in (20-cm) cake pans with parchment paper cut to fit.

3. Put the butter into your mixing bowl, making sure that it is really soft and creamy by giving it a good stir with a wooden spoon or switching on the mixer for a couple of minutes. Then add the sugar and whisk it for a minute or two.

4. Crack the eggs into a small bowl and then add them with the flour, baking powder, and milk to the mixing bowl. Beat the mixture together until it is completely blended and smooth.

5. Spoon the mixture into the 2 pans and level the top with a spatula or spoon.

6. Put the cakes on the middle rack of the hot oven and bake for about 25–30 minutes. NO peeking for at least 20 minutes!

Take care, it's hot!

7. When the cake is ready it will feel springy when you touch the top and should have a gap between the cake and the pan. Poke a skewer or toothpick into the cake — it should come out clean.

8. Leave the cakes to cool in the pans for 5 minutes, then carefully turn them out onto a wire rack. The pans could still burn you, so it's best to have some help.

9. Peel off the paper and leave the cakes to cool.

10. Sandwich the cakes together with your chosen filling and decorate the top, if you like. Get ready for the compliments!

Cold air rushes into the oven when you open the door and might cause your cake to sink.

Turn the page for some great ideas.

Double Choc Cake

3 tbsp unsweetened cocoa

3 tbsp boiling water

scant 1 cup (200 g) softened butter

1 cup (200 g) superfine sugar

4 medium eggs

1½ cups (200 g) self-rising flour

1 tsp baking powder

2 tbsp milk

½ cup (100 g) dark or milk chocolate chips

You can follow THE Cake Recipe (turn back a page) with 2 extra steps:

- At step 3, put the unsweetened cocoa into a mug, pour over 3 tablespoons boiling water, and stir to a thick paste. Leave to cool while you beat together the butter and sugar.

- Add the cocoa paste to the cake mixture at the same time as the eggs, flour, and baking powder in step 4. Stir in the chocolate chips just before you put the mixture in the pan.

Lemon or Orange Cake

1 orange or 1 lemon

scant 1 cup (200 g) softened butter

1 cup (200 g) superfine sugar

4 medium eggs

scant 1½ cups (200 g) self-rising flour

1 tsp baking powder

2 tbsp milk

You can follow THE Cake Recipe (turn back a page) with just 1 extra step:

- Grate the zest of your orange or lemon and add it to the bowl with the butter at the beginning of step 3.

That's all there is to it.

Great sandwiched together with about 5 tbsp marmalade or lemon curd.

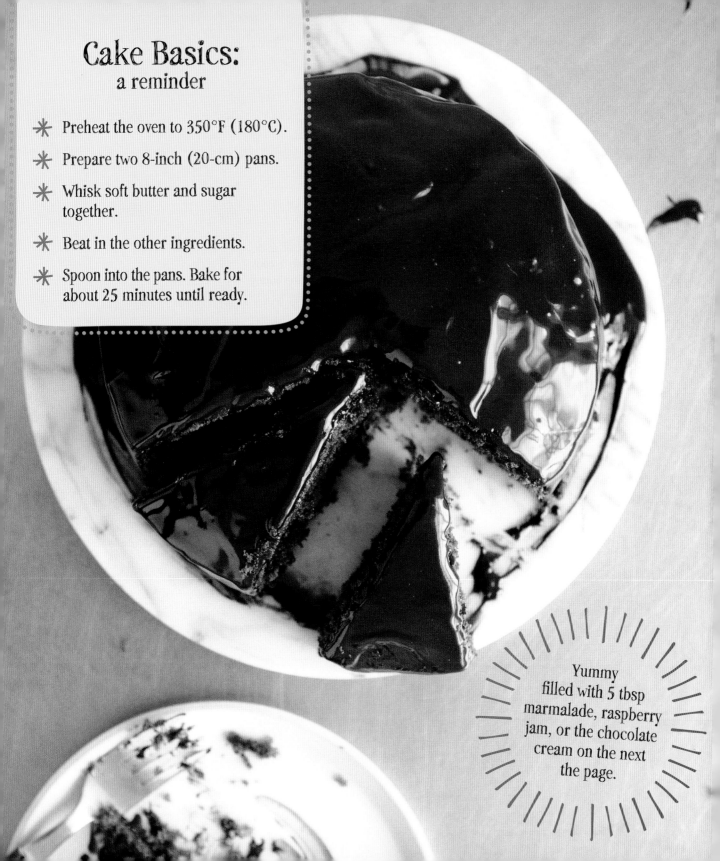

Cake Basics:
a reminder

* Preheat the oven to 350°F (180°C).
* Prepare two 8-inch (20-cm) pans.
* Whisk soft butter and sugar together.
* Beat in the other ingredients.
* Spoon into the pans. Bake for about 25 minutes until ready.

Yummy filled with 5 tbsp marmalade, raspberry jam, or the chocolate cream on the next the page.

THE CAKE Fillings

Use a palette knife or spatula to spread your chosen filling on one half of your cake.

JAMMY

4 tablespoons jam, marmalade, or lemon curd make a simple but very delicious filling.

FRUITY

A pint of raspberries, blueberries, or strawberries and a tablespoon of sugar are perfect with either creamy filling.

CREAMY

1 cup (250 ml) heavy cream can be whipped until thick and just holding its shape. Stir in 1 tablespoon superfine sugar.

OR

$^2/_3$ cup (150 g) mascarpone cheese whisked with $^2/_3$ cup (150 g) fromage frais, 1 tablespoon superfine sugar and 1 teaspoon vanilla extract.

CHOCOLATEY

$^2/_3$ cup (150 ml) heavy cream

Make sure it's heavy; light cream may separate when you heat it.

$5^1/_2$ oz (150 g) dark or milk chocolate

Break the chocolate into pieces and place in a small saucepan with the cream.

Put the pan over low heat and stir with a wooden spoon until the chocolate has completely melted. Don't let it boil.

Now take the pan off the heat and stir until the mixture looks shiny and thick.

Pour the chocolate into a bowl and leave to cool for about 15–30 minutes until it thickens just enough to spread. In hot weather you may need to put it in the fridge.

Don't whisk for too long or the cream will go grainy and lumpy.

THE CAKE
Toppings

To sprinkle or spread over the cake.

ICING

2 cups (225 g) confectioners' sugar

2 tbsp HOT liquid
Yes, it's a tiny amount, but just watch, it will be enough.
The liquid can be water, milk, lemon juice, orange juice, raspberry juice, coffee
(1 tablespoon instant coffee to 2 tablespoons boiling water), or chocolate
(1 tablespoon cocoa powder to 2 tablespoons boiling water)

Mix the sugar and your chosen liquid with a fork until smooth.

A couple of drops of food coloring will transform your icing.

SUGARY

A sprinkling of superfine sugar is a classic.

CHOCOLATEY

If you want a chocolate filling AND topping, follow the recipe on the left, using 1 cup (250 ml) heavy cream and 9 oz (250 g) chocolate.

A warm spatula makes spreading icing or ganache easier.

CREAMY

Use the second creamy option on the left.

Double the recipe if you want enough for the inside AND top.

Try to track down the natural colors you can find in the shops nowadays.

10

Just Desserts

sweet endings

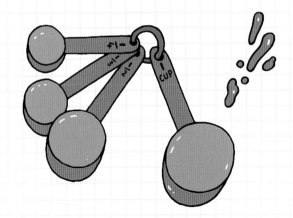

Tropical Fruit Skewers

MAKES 4

Unless you want a bonfire.

Remember to soak the wooden skewers in water while you prepare your fruit.

---

1 small pineapple

1 ripe mango

1 lime + 1 lime, to serve

2 medium bananas

1 passion fruit

2 tbsp light brown sugar

4 large or 8 small skewers, soaked in water

---

1 Cutting the pineapple may require some help.

2 Now prepare your mango — there's a trick to this too!

3 Zest the lime and squeeze the juice into a bowl.

4 Peel and chop the bananas into 2-in (5-cm) chunks, and add them to the lime juice in the bowl along with the lime zest.

5 Thread the fruit onto the soaked wooden skewers in alternate chunks.

6 Cut the passion fruit in half and slice the lime for serving into quarters.

7 Line an ovenproof pan with foil and lay the skewers on the foil.

8 Preheat the broiler about 10 minutes before serving.

9 Sprinkle the skewers with the sugar and place under the hot broiler for about 5–10 minutes. The idea is to toast and scorch the top of the fruit rather than cook it.

10 Serve the skewers straightaway with a squeeze of passion fruit over the top and a small wedge of lime on the side.

How to Prepare Mango

The fruit naturally lies flat with the seed, so turn it onto its side.

You need to cut the flesh from either side of the pit with a serrated fruit knife.

Now cut a square grid in the flesh with your knife, without cutting through the skin. Leave the squares about 1¼ in (3 cm) across if you are making the skewers.

Push the skin inside out for a kind of hedgehog effect and carefully slice off the cubes.

1

2

5

How to
Prepare Pineapple

First you need to cut off the leaves and the base. Then slice off the skin, taking away as little flesh as possible. You will be left with the little eyes.

Use a small serrated knife to saw out the diagonal lines of the eyes.

Now cut the pineapple in half and then into quarters and slice off the tough inner core.

Cut the pineapple into cubes (about 2 in/5 cm). Or just cut the fruit into long strips.

10

Fruit Bowl

Fruit doesn't just taste great, it also makes you look and feel healthy, and helps fight off diseases too.

Smoothies and juices are packed with goodness (vitamins and minerals), but eating, rather than drinking, fruit is even better for you. That's because the fiber (the solid stuff) gives your intestines a keep-fit routine; it keeps them busy for longer so you feel full and energized for longer too. Fiber also keeps food moving through your body, helping you to have a regular poo.

When we're talking about food, we think of fruit as sweet and vegetables as savory, but scientifically that's just not the case...

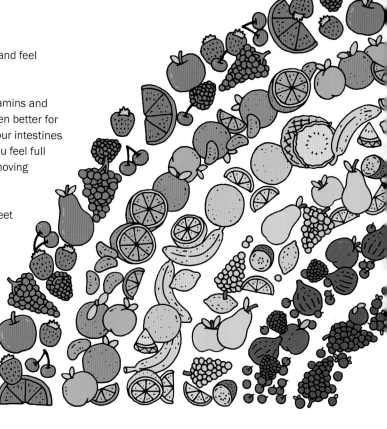

Do you know your fruit from your veg?

Tomato   Plum   Rhubarb   Olive   Pumpkin

Which of the foods above is the odd one out?

The rhubarb: it's the only vegetable! All the others are technically fruits – a fruit is the part of the plant that holds the seeds. That means that cucumbers, eggplants, peppers, and runner beans are fruits too. Can you think of any more?

CHALLENGE

Try to eat a fruit or vegetable from every color group every day for a week – it could become a habit!

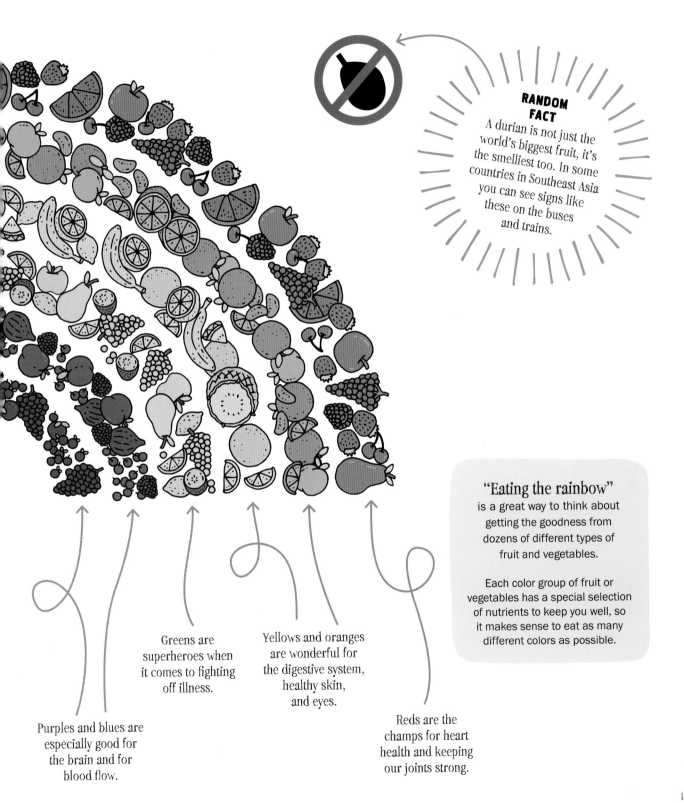

"Eating the rainbow" is a great way to think about getting the goodness from dozens of different types of fruit and vegetables.

Each color group of fruit or vegetables has a special selection of nutrients to keep you well, so it makes sense to eat as many different colors as possible.

Greens are superheroes when it comes to fighting off illness.

Yellows and oranges are wonderful for the digestive system, healthy skin, and eyes.

Purples and blues are especially good for the brain and for blood flow.

Reds are the champs for heart health and keeping our joints strong.

Chocolate Sauce

SERVES 8

You couldn't have a cookbook without a chocolate sauce! There's no point in trying to make a healthy version; let's face it, it's a special treat.

Try dipping pretzels for a salty-sweet sensation.

5½ oz (150 g) semisweet chocolate

2 tbsp light corn syrup or maple syrup

1¼ cups (300 ml) heavy cream

1 Break the chocolate into small pieces and put it into a saucepan with the syrup and cream.

2 Place the pan on low heat and stir with a wooden spoon to gently melt the chocolate.

3 Serve the sauce warm. You can make it ahead and reheat gently before serving.

4 Pour over vanilla ice cream or pancakes. Or serve in warm bowls and dip in strawberries, banana chunks, and other fruit, like a chocolate fondue.

You can't hurry chocolate; it will separate and go horribly grainy if you heat it above about 120°F (49°C).

Frozen Banana Sticks

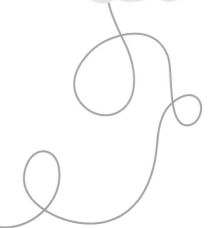

HEAVEN!

Magic — no cooking required and the frozen bananas have a really creamy texture!

1 small, ripe banana per person

juice of 1 lemon (will be enough for about 6)

chocolate sauce (see above) – optional

wooden popsicle sticks

1 Peel the bananas and chop off the pointed ends.

2 Push the popsicle stick carefully up the center of the banana. Now brush with lemon juice to stop the banana from going brown and freeze in a plastic freezer bag.

3 Leave for a minimum of 5 hours.

4 Try dipping in the chocolate sauce.

Elderflower Jello

SERVES 4

KITCHEN FACTS
Gelatin is not suitable for vegetarians; it's made from collagen found in cow and pig bones and hides. Vegetarians can use agar-agar flakes to set jello.

Elderflower syrup is popular in many European countries. It makes a crystal clear jello that works like a magnifying glass, making the fruit in the middle look huge. If you can't find it, use a fruit-flavored beverage syrup (such as lemon) in its place.

1 package (1 tbsp) powdered gelatin

2/3 cup (150 ml) elderflower syrup or lemon syrup

1 1/2 cups (350 ml) water

1 1/3 cups (200 g) whole berries such as blueberries, raspberries, or strawberries, washed

1 Soak the gelatin in enough cold water to cover and set aside.

2 Meanwhile, mix your elderflower syrup and water together in a large jug. It should taste sweeter than you would usually drink it because you will be serving it chilled. !!!!!

3 Heat up about a quarter of the elderflower mixture in a large saucepan. You don't want it boiling — just hot. Remove the pan from the heat.

4 Add the gelatin to the hot elderflower mixture in the pan. Stir with a wooden spoon until the gelatin completely dissolves and disappears.

5 Add the rest of the cold elderflower liquid to the pan and give it all a stir. Transfer to a pitcher.

6 Now, you choose. You can pour the jello into molds to turn out later or simply serve the jello from glasses. Half fill your glasses or molds with the elderflower mixture.

7 Chop the fruit into smaller pieces if necessary and spoon in half of the fruit into your molds. The fruit will bob to the top. Pop the jellies into the fridge to set and keep the pitcher of unset mixture to one side.

8 After about an hour, when the fruit is just set in the jellies, pour in the rest of the elderflower mixture from the pan and drop in the remaining berries.

9 Chill in the fridge for a few more hours until set and then serve.

Cold food numbs your taste buds.

Metal molds work well because they warm through quickly.

MAGIC!

Turning out your jello

Carefully dip the jello molds into a bowl of hot water, one at a time, taking care that the water doesn't go in the jello. The idea is to melt the outside of the jello. Turn the mold upside down onto a plate and WOBBLE it. If it won't come out, try dipping again.

Greasing the molds with vegetable oil will help later on.

Fruity Crumble

There's nothing flashy about a crumble, but it's a great dessert; you can use whatever seasonal fruit is available and everyone seems to love it.

You'll need an ovenproof dish about 10 in (25 cm) square and 2 in (5 cm) deep.

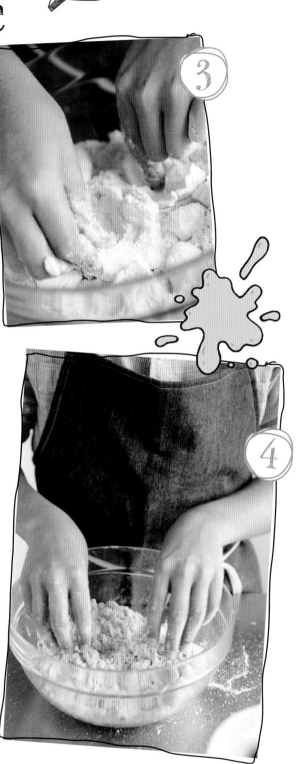

The Crunchy Top

²/₃ cup (140 g) chilled butter

1½ cups (200 g) all-purpose flour

pinch of salt

½ cup (100 g) superfine sugar, or light brown muscovado sugar, or a mix of the two

1 Preheat the oven to 400°F (200°C).

2 Chop the cold butter into small squares and drop them into a large mixing bowl with the flour and salt.

3 Give everything a quick stir with your hands and then rub the pieces of butter into the flour using your fingertips.

4 Once the mixture looks like bread crumbs, with no big lumps of butter, you can stir the sugar in with a spoon.

5 Put the crumble mixture into the fridge if you have room while you prepare the filling.

The Fruity Bottom

The fruit will depend on the season and what you love eating but here are a few suggestions.

You'll see a pattern:
2 lb (900 g) prepared fruit so you can experiment with plums, pears, nectarines, and raspberries and try all sorts of different combinations.

For Apple Crumble

2 lb (900 g) firm green apples such as Granny Smith or pippin or, best of all, a mixture of the two

1 tbsp sugar

a pinch of ground cinnamon

1 Peel, core, and cut the apples into chunks or rough slices.

2 Put the apples into your ovenproof dish and sprinkle over the sugar and cinnamon. Tumble the fruit over with your fingers to mix.

3 Spoon the crumble mix over the fruit and bake in the oven for 30 minutes until golden.

For Rhubarb Crumble

2 lb (900 g) rhubarb

3 tbsp ground almonds

3 tbsp sugar

1 Cut the leaves and any ragged ends from the rhubarb and then chop into logs, just about the size of your little finger.

2 Sprinkle the ground almonds into the bottom of the ovenproof dish.

3 Lay the rhubarb over the top and scatter over the sugar.

4 Spoon the crumble mix over the fruit and bake in the oven for 30 minutes until golden.

For Blackberry and Apple Crumble

A good reason to get out picking

Follow the recipe above; just replace about 7 oz (200 g) of your apples with 1⅓ cups (200 g) washed blackberries.

For Strawberry and Rhubarb Crumble

Use the recipe above, swapping about 2 cups (300 g) strawberries for 10½ oz (300 g) of the rhubarb.

1 Hull the strawberries and cut them into halves or quarters.

Remove the green leafy bit.

2 Add to the dish at the same time as the rhubarb.

Serve the crumble with vanilla
ice cream or heavy cream.

Index

DEDICATION

For Imi, a great cook in the making and my favorite daughter ever!

ACKNOWLEDGMENTS

Huge Thanks:

To all of the children who've inspired and made this book happen, especially my gorgeous Imi; you did a great job of cooking your way through virtually every recipe and giving me "plenty" of advice along the way. To the exceptionally keen school friends who've taken part in our "Monday Night Cooking Club," you created some fabulous suppers and helped narrow down the recipes for the final cut. And to all the pupils at Hotwells Primary School, your curiosity and creativity sparked so many ideas during our cooking sessions.

To the great team at Pavilion, especially my editor, Emily Preece-Morrison. I love working with you; you always understand where I'm headed, help steer the way, and then do the most incredible job of tailoring all the ideas and excess text into a stunning book. You're a legend. To Kathy Steer for meticulous copyediting and Laura Russell and Clare Clewley for doing the most amazing job with the design and layout, you've made the recipes come to life.

To everyone involved with the shoot, you've achieved the engaging, fun, and informative look that I so hoped for; Rob Wicks, you set the ball rolling with your gorgeous shots; Wei Tang, you brought your special magic into the styling and were so fab to work with too; Valerie Berry, you not only produced some gorgeous-looking food but did such a great job with the young 'uns, even throwing in a bit of reflexology when required; Alex James Gray, your organization and attention to detail is second to none; Deirdre Rooney, you absolutely captured the spirit of kids cooking with your beautiful photographs. To the very patient, talented and photogenic young cooks; Imogen Bassett, Alpha Djenguet, Jonas and Piers Clarke, Sam and Maddie Fisher, Annabelle Frainer-Law, Ethan Goodman-Ancell, Joe and Charlie Ives, Matthew Jervis, Rhys Morrison, Theo Nearney, Saskia Portman, Dylan and Jake Turner.

To Damien Weighill, your quirky illustrations are truly inspired and give the entire book so much energy; you nailed it.

Lastly, I am so grateful to my now husband, Peter and the rest of my family and friends who've listened to me rambling, stressing (not that often) and enthusing about this book for many, many months; we got there.

weldonowen

Published in North America by Weldon Owen
1045 Sansome Street, San Francisco, CA 94111
www.weldonowen.com
Weldon Owen is a division of Bonnier Publishing USA

This edition published in 2017

First published in the United Kingdom in 2016 by Pavilion

Text © Jenny Chandler, 2016
Design and layout © Pavilion Books Company Ltd, 2016
Photography and illustrations © Pavilion Books Company Ltd, 2016

The moral rights of the author have been asserted.

Library of Congress Cataloging-in-Publication data is available

ISBN: 978-1-68188-187-4
10 9 8 7 6 5 4 3 2 1

Reproduction by Mission, Hong Kong
Printed and bound by 1010 Printing International Ltd, China